The ABC's of FRUITS AND VEGETABLES AND BEYOND

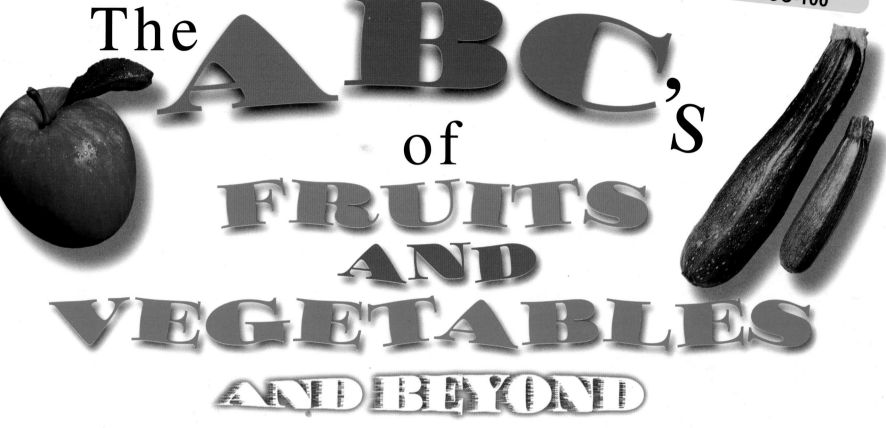

Delicious Alphabet Poems *plus* Food, Facts, and Fun for Everyone

by

Steve Charney & David Goldbeck

Illustrations by Maria Burgaleta Larson

Ceres Press
A Peach Fuzz Book
Woodstock, New York

In memory of Ilse Goldbeck, who knew that tomatoes are fruits and let David eat cabbage raw because he liked it better than cooked cabbage.

Copyright © 2007 Steve Charney and David Goldbeck.
Recipes copyright © 2007 Nikki and David Goldbeck

10 digit 1-886101-07-8
13 digit 978-1-886101-07-4

LCCN 00-190593

Publisher's Cataloging-in-Publication

Charney, Steve.
    The ABC's of fruits and vegetables and beyond: delicious alphabet poems plus / by Steve Charney and David Goldbeck; illustrations by Maria Burgaleta Larson. – 1st ed.
    p.cm
    Includes bibliographical references.
    SUMMARY: A is for applesauce, B is for bananas, and so on, in this rhyming introduction to fruits and vegetables, with recipes, food facts, and literature links appended.
    ISBN: 1-886101-07-8

    1. Cookery (Fruit)—Juvenile literature.
    2. Cookery (Vegetables)—Juvenile literature.
    3. Fruit—Juvenile literature. 4. Vegetables—Juvenile literature. 5. English language—Alphabet—Juvenile literature. I. Goldbeck, David. II. Larson, Maria Burgaleta. III. Title.

TX811.C43 2007   641.5'123
QBI00-239

ACKNOWLEDGEMENTS

Steve would like to thank his mother for getting him to eat his vegetables as a child and his brother Ken for getting him to eat them as a man. He would also like to thank Elise, Dad, Louise, Jerry, David, Nikki, Mayita, Mickey, Bob, Marcy, Hank, Jency...and you.

David thanks Steve Charney and Nikki Goldbeck for their faith in this project. He is also grateful to Judy Fishetti, Joanne Sackett, Rick Rhoder, Daphne Jackson, Tamara Katzowitz, Gayla Pearson, Janice King, Jayna Nelson, Melody Kauff, Elena M. Byrne, Barry Samuels, Lewis Gardner, Mark Larson, Maria Burgaleta Larson, Naomi Schmidt, Sandy King and Helen Hughes for the support each provided.

Special thanks to Fern Gale Estrow, MS, RD, CDN for her support of this project.

Ceres Press
PO Box 87 Dept. ABC
Woodstock, NY 12498 USA
(845) 679-5573
cem620@aol.com
www.HealthyHighways.com

Concept: David Goldbeck
Produced by: David Goldbeck
ABC's and other poems: Steve Charney
Beyond the ABC's: David Goldbeck
Food Editor: Nikki Goldbeck
Editor: Lewis Gardner
Illustrations: Maria Burgaleta Larson
Cover and Page Design: Mark Larson Design
                         www.mlarson.com
Additional Graphic Design: Naomi Graphics
                         www.naomigraphics.com

PART ONE

The

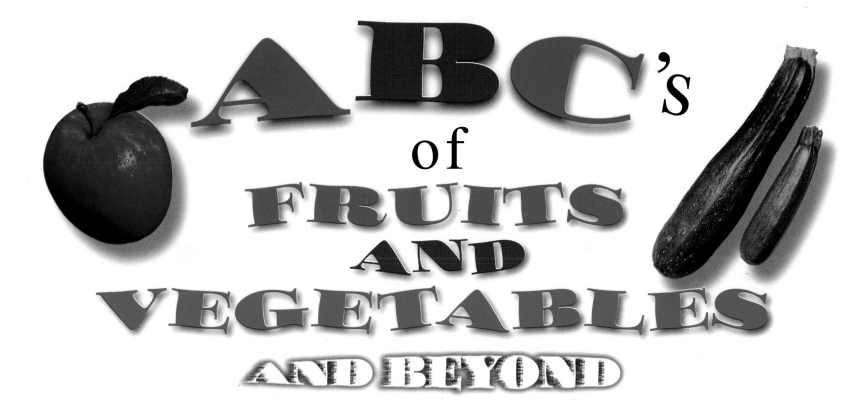

ABC's
of
FRUITS
AND
VEGETABLES
AND BEYOND

**is
also for:**

acorn squash

apricot

artichoke

asparagus

avocado

Let's start with **A** for applesauce.
We'll show the apples who's the boss –
We'll squeeze and squish and squash and squush
Until the apples turn to mush.

B is for bananas.

The U.S. loves this fruit –
It certainly is "a peeling"
In its pretty yellow suit.

is
also for:

cabbage

cantaloupe

celery

cherries

corn

C

is for the carrots
That rabbits like to munch.
They eat them 'cause they love the taste –
Me... I like the crunch!

Appreciate the **D** for date,

A desert fruit found in Kuwait.

Let's travel there – we'll bring a plate –

Do you want to pick the date?

E is
also for:

endive

escarole

E is for the eggplant,
A fruit with purple skin.
Do you suppose an eggplant
Comes from a purple hen?

fennel

fig

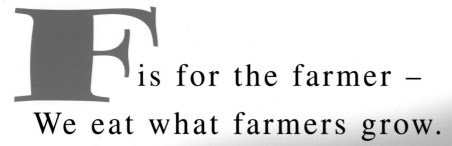is for the farmer –
We eat what farmers grow.
They turn the dirt and plant the seeds
With a hearty hoe-hoe-hoe!

G
is
also for:

garlic

grapefruit

green beans

Gee, we love those yummy grapes –
The juicy taste, the groovy shapes.
They hang in bunches, that's their trick
To make them easier to pick.

H
is
also for:

honeydew

H is for the herbs on pizza—
We'll make the pie taste nice
With basil
and oregano.
Let's have
a second
slice!

ACCURACY ALERT ☞ Don't get us wrong – herbs are not what most people would call a vegetable. Herbs are used in foods to make them taste and look better. Actually, some herbs such as parsley, dill, and basil are often eaten just like a vegetable.

I is for the Idaho,
A potato Idahoans grow.
Can Ohians in　Ohio
Grow Idahos?　Ida know.

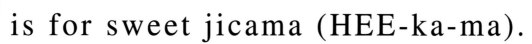

J is for sweet jicama (HEE-ka-ma).
They're eaten sliced or whole.
If you pronounce the J like H,
You're speaking
Español!

K

is
also for:

kale

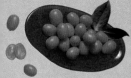

kumquats

 is for the kiwi –
It's green and sweet within.
We never would have guessed it
By its brown
and fuzzy
skin.

L

is
also for:

leek

lettuce

lime

Lemons start with L, you know.
You may not want to eat one though.
The lemon has a sour taste –
One bite makes YOU sour-faced!

M

is
also for:

melon

mint

mushroom

mustard
greens

M is for the mango,
Which Mayans found divine.
They often danced the tango
While they ate them
with a lime.

The nectarine begins with  N.
It's like a peach with smoother skin.
Nectar means a drink from heaven –
With that in mind, we'll buy eleven!

is
also for:

okra

olive

onion

orange

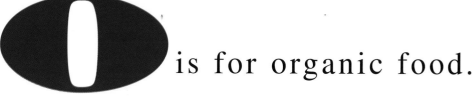

O is for organic food.
It's grown the natural way.
Some say that harmful chemicals
Should take a holiday!

P is
also for:

papaya

peach

pear

pepper

pineapple

P

is for the fresh green peas.

Don't eat them on the rolling seas –

It makes the captain mad as heck

To see peas rolling off the deck!

Q is for the sour quince.
We tried one once but haven't since.
It's better in a jam or fritter –
By itself it's much too bitter.

R

is
also for:

raspberries

rhubarb

rutabaga

R is for the radish.

Radishes are reddish,

And Russians really relish

A radish when they're famished.

s

is
also for:

scallions

spinach

squash

strawberry

S is for the squiggly sprout.
We like to watch the sprout grow out.
From beans as tiny
as this  o
They
Grow
and
GROW
and
GROW
and
GROW!

T
is
also for:

tangelo

tangerine

turnips

T is for tomato.

Did you know that it's a fruit?

Some say that it's a vegetable,

Which causes a dispute.

U

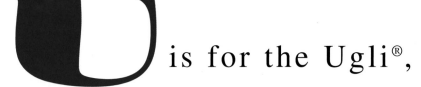

U is for the Ugli®,
A large round wrinkly fruit.
Don't judge it by its outer skin –
Inside it's kind of cute!

V

is for vanilla bean.
It's tasted more than it is seen,
Because a kid
would surely groan
To find beans in
her ice cream
cone!

ACCURACY ALERT ☞ We don't want you to get the wrong idea – vanilla is NOT a fruit or a vegetable. It's a flavoring. A flavoring is anything used to change the taste of food. Other favorite flavorings are chocolate, ginger, cinnamon and garlic.

is
also for:

watercress

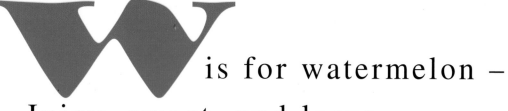 is for watermelon –
Juicy, sweet, and large.
I found one in my garden
As big as our garage!

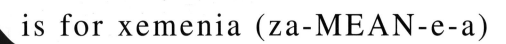

X is for xemenia (za-MEAN-e-a)

Don't get this fruit too riled.

He's not found
at the fruit stand,
So hunt him
in the wild.

is
also for:

yellow squash

A yam's a  Yam – there's no confusion –
The wise have come to this conclusion.
Say Einstein, Newton, Marx and Plato:
A yam is NOT a sweet potato!

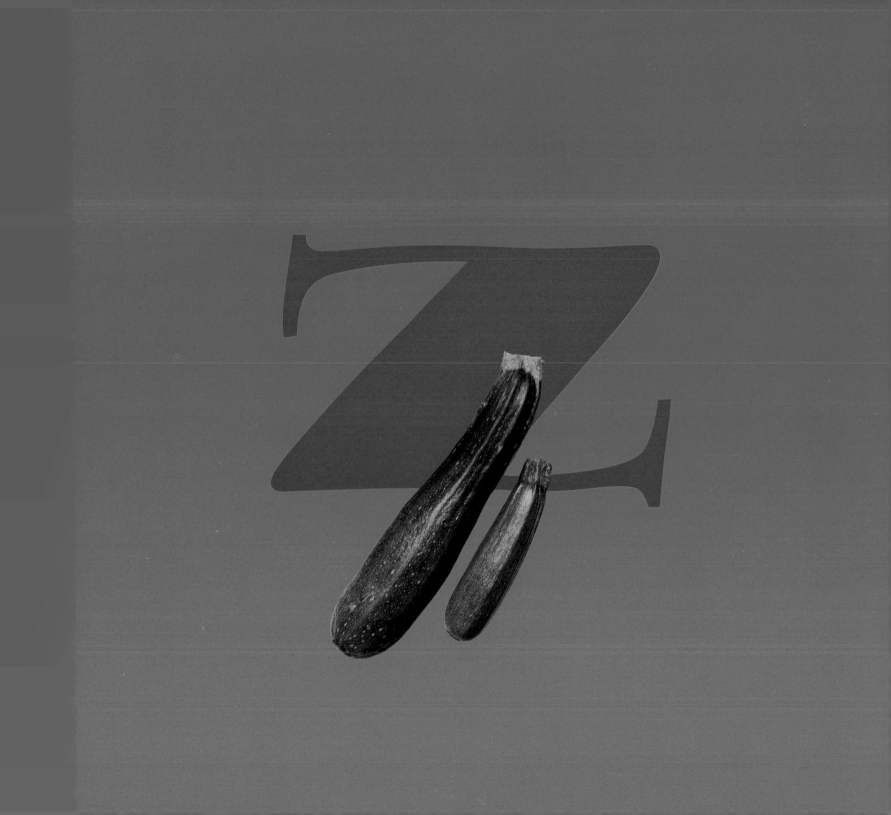

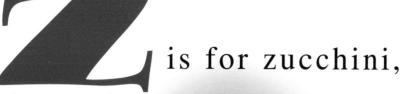**Z** is for zucchini,
A word to flabbergast.
"Zucchini with linguini"–
Try to say that ten times fast!

Do you know when we call something a fruit?

A fruit is the part of a plant or tree that contains the seeds. A fruit is usually juicy and fleshy. Some fruits, such as tomatoes and eggplants, are eaten like vegetables.

These are all fruits. Do you see the seeds?

Apple

Kiwi

Cantaloupe

Papaya

Grapefruit

Peach

Strawberry

tomato

Watermelon

Do you know when we call something a vegetable?

A vegetable is any part of a plant other than the fruit that is used for food. These are leaves, buds, flowers, shoots, roots, and tubers.

BUDS

New plant growth is called a bud. Brussels sprouts and red cabbage are good examples of this kind of vegetable.

STEMS and SHOOTS

Vegetables can also be plant stems and shoots such as celery and asparagus.

FLOWERS

Broccoli, cauliflowers, and globe artichokes are, in fact, flowers.

ROOTS

Roots supply us with a wide selection of vegetables. These include the radish, carrot, parsnip, and beet.

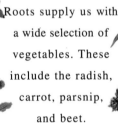

LEAVES

The leaves of plants are one kind of vegetable. These include lettuce, cabbage, and spinach.

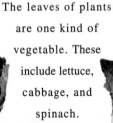

TUBERS

A tuber is a swollen part of a plant's stem. Many people think a potato is a root vegetable, but it is actually a tuber.

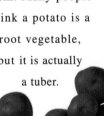

PART TWO

BEYOND THE ABC's

FOOD, FACTS, AND FUN FOR EVERYONE

Look for these icons. They will guide you through these pages

 ABOUT
Learn more.

Help needed for this activity.

 OOH!
OOH= Out Of Hand
You can eat this food raw.

True Food Fact
You will be amazed!

 **Read On**
Read more about it.

Beyond

ABOUT The apples we eat today come from apples that were grown more than two million years ago! At first, people ate wild apples picked in the forest. These apples tasted bitter and were only the size of a strawberry. About 10,000 years ago, people started planting and growing better apples. This period is called the Stone Age because of the kinds of tools that were used. The apples that are grown today are relatives of Stone Age apples, but they're much bigger and sweeter. Their skins can be red to lemony yellow to yellow-green. Apples are best during the fall, when newly picked. In the market, buy firm, brightly colored apples with a fresh smell. You can keep apples for a long time in a cool place.

Recipes:

ABC Applesauce

apples
honey or maple syrup
cinnamon

1. Using a vegetable peeler, remove the apple skins.

2. Cut the apples into pieces. Throw away the seeds and the core.

3. Place the apples in a saucepan with ¼ cup of water. Cook for about 15 minutes or until the apples are soft enough to mash with a fork or potato masher.

4. Remove the pot from the heat. Mash the apples.

5. Eat the applesauce as it is, or sweeten it to taste with a little honey or maple syrup and cinnamon. Serve warm or cold.

Applewiches

apples
orange juice
peanut butter or cheddar cheese

1. Use one apple for each person. Remove the center core from the apple. Slice the fruit into rings.

2. Dip the apple slices into a little orange juice to keep them from turning brown.

3. Put a spoonful of peanut butter or a slice of cheese on half of the apple rings. Place a second apple ring on top to make a sandwich.

4. Eat applewiches right away or wrap them in foil and put them in the refrigerator for later. Eat them before 24 hours have passed.

How do you like these apples?

There may be as many as 7,000 different kinds of apples! Only about 100 are available in markets. Here are some common ones. How many have you eaten? Delicious, golden delicious, winesap, Rome beauty, Granny Smith, Braeburn, Fuji, Cortland, stayman, Asian pear, gravenstein, Ida red, Jonathan, lady, macoun, McIntosh, pippin, Rhode Island greening, Royal gala.

A person who is THE APPLE OF YOUR EYE is someone you like

How To Keep An Apple From Browning

Apples get brown once they are cut. There is a way to stop it from happening. Here is an experiment that shows that it works.

What you need: an apple, lemon juice.

1. Cut the apple into 4 pieces.

2. Sprinkle lemon juice on two of the quarters. Put one with and one without lemon juice in the refrigerator. Leave the other two on the counter.

3. What happens? The untreated apple on the counter turns brown first. The apple with the lemon juice that was put in the refrigerator stays white the longest.

Read On

FIRST APPLE

by Ching Young Russell

(Boyd Mills Press)

This story is about a young Chinese girl's dream to taste an apple and buy one as a gift for her grandmother.

The Joke Bag

Q: How do you know that an elephant has been in your refrigerator?

A: There are footprints in the applesauce!

Beyond B

ABOUT Bananas grow in bunches. A bunch of bananas is called a hand. Each banana is a finger. One banana plant can have as many as 100 fingers. While most fruit is picked when it's ready to eat, bananas are cut down when they're still green. Bananas ripen off the plant – they turn yellow and become tasty and sweet. There are hundreds of kinds of bananas, but the one called yellow Cavendish is the most popular in the U.S. In the market, bananas will be green to yellow, some with tiny brown specks. The yellow ones are ready to eat, but those with a few brown specks are the sweetest. Green bananas will ripen at home. Do you know that they will ripen faster if you put them in a bag? Some people think bananas should not be put in the refrigerator. But ripe bananas can be refrigerated for a few days. The peel will turn brown, but the inside will be splendid.

Recipes:

Banana Soft Serve

A cool treat!

1. Peel as many bananas as you need, so each person has one banana.

2. Put the bananas in a plastic freezer bag. Squeeze out all the air and seal the bag tightly. Place it in the freezer.

3. Just before serving, remove the bananas from the freezer and break them into chunks. Put them in the work bowl of a food processor. Turn the machine on and let it run until the bananas break up. Continue until the mashed banana becomes creamy, light in color, and whipped with air.

5. Spoon the whipped banana into bowls, paper cups, or cones, and eat it right away.

Monkeys in a Blanket

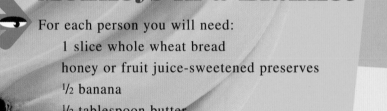

For each person you will need:
1 slice whole wheat bread
honey or fruit juice-sweetened preserves
1/2 banana
1/2 tablespoon butter
cinnamon

1. Set the oven or toaster oven to 400°F. and let it warm up.

2. Cut the crusts off the bread.. Flatten the bread with a rolling pin, or by pressing down hard with the palm of your hand.

3. Spread a thin layer of honey or preserves on the bread. Place the banana half on the bread. Roll the bread over the banana so that it is completely covered.

4. Place the butter in a baking dish and put it in the oven or toaster oven for a minute to melt. Using a potholder, carefully take the pan out of the oven and place it on a heatproof surface.

5. Roll each "Monkey in a Blanket" in the melted butter. Set them side by side in the baking pan. Sprinkle with a lot of cinnamon.

6. Bake for 15 minutes, until the outside is crisp and the banana is hot and creamy. Let the "Monkey" cool down a little before you take a bite.

ABOUT the B poem

Americans eat more bananas than any other fruit. Their next four favorites are apples, watermelons, oranges, and cantaloupes.

How do you like these bananas?

Some markets sell a variety of bananas. They all taste just a little bit different. Some bananas have red skin. Small, chubby bananas may be called dwarf bananas. Another, the banana apple, has an apple-like taste. One that isn't sweet, the plantain, is used for cooking. How many have you tasted?

True Food Fact

Bananas don't grow on trees! What people call banana trees are really the world's biggest herbs. They can grow up to 25 feet high. You can discover more about herbs at the letter "H."

If you're the TOP BANANA you are the person in charge

The Joke Bag

A woman is riding on a train. Across from her a man is peeling bananas, putting sugar and salt on them, and throwing them in the garbage can. The woman says to the man "Why are you putting sugar and salt on bananas and throwing them out?" The man replies, "I HATE bananas with sugar and salt on them!"

www.bananamuseum.com
See more than 4,000 objects at the Banana Museum.

Read On

SWEET, SWEET FIG BANANA
by Phyllis Gershator
(Albert Whitman & Co.)

If you are a new reader, this tale of a boy in the Caribbean who plants a banana tree, and shares his harvest to repay the kindness of others, is for you.

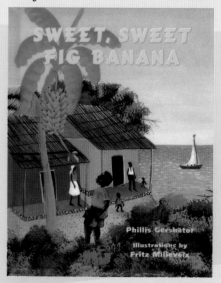

SWEET, SWEET FIG BANANA
Phyllis Gershator
Illustrations by Fritz Millevoix

Beyond C

ABOUT

Carrots are a root vegetable. This means they grow underground. Some other root vegetables are beets, radishes, turnips, and parsnips. Carrots have been around for over 2,000 years. In the market, you'll find carrots with and without their green leafy tops, as well as baby carrots. All carrots should be firm and smooth. Don't buy those with cracks or any that have begun to soften. The best carrots are young and skinny. Tiny baby carrots are very tender, but they are not as tasty as full-grown ones. If you buy carrots with the tops, remove them as soon as possible. The carrots will keep longer.

OOH! Baby carrots should be rinsed off and regular carrots scraped with a peeler before eating.

Recipe:

Carrot Cookies

It's too bad rabbits can't bake. This recipe makes about 40 cookies.

1 cup whole wheat flour
1 teaspoon baking powder
1/8 teaspoon salt
1 cup rolled oats
1/4 cup sunflower seeds
1/4 cup walnut pieces
1/4 cup raisins
1 cup shredded carrots
1/2 cup honey
1/2 cup canola oil
1/4 teaspoon vanilla extract

1. Set the oven to 375°F. and let it warm up.

2. In a large bowl, mix together the flour, baking powder, salt, oats, sunflower seeds, walnut pieces, raisins, and shredded carrots.

3. In a different bowl, beat together the honey, oil, and vanilla.

4. Add the honey mixture to the flour mixture. Stir until they are well mixed and the flour isn't dry anymore.

5. Dampen a paper towel with oil. Use it to wipe a cookie sheet until it is coated with oil.

6. Take a rounded teaspoonful of cookie dough at a time. Place it on the oiled cookie sheet. When you have used up all the dough, pat each ball down. Flatten it with your fingers, so the cookies hold together.

7. Place the cookies in the oven. Bake them for 10 to 12 minutes, until they are light brown.

8. Using a potholder, remove the cookie sheet from the oven. Let the cookies rest for 1 minute. Using a spatula, carefully move the cookies to a wire rack, so they can cool.

Recipe: Sweet Orange Carrot Coins

This side dish will make you rich. Coins for four people.

- 1 pound carrots
- 1 tablespoon butter
- ½ cup orange juice
- 1 tablespoon honey

1. Using a vegetable peeler, remove the carrot peels. Wash the carrots and slice them into pieces the size of a coin

2. Melt the butter in a large skillet. Add the carrot coins and stir, so they are covered with the butter.

3. Add the orange juice, cover the pan, and cook over medium heat for 10 minutes, or until the carrots are just tender.

4. Stir in the honey, turn up the heat, and let the orange juice boil quickly – until it is almost all gone.

5. Put some carrot coins on your plate, and enjoy their sweet orange taste.

 grimmway.com/Consumers

Click on "At Home" to find carrot trivia and the Fun Zone.

The Joke Bag

Q: How do you catch a rabbit?

A: Hide in a bush and make a noise like a carrot.

Carrot Tricks

Make these cool "carrot curls" for your salads. Pick a medium size carrot. Wash it. Use a vegetable peeler to make thin, lengthwise carrot slices. Roll each slice up and stick in a toothpick to hold it together. Place in a bowl of ice water for an hour or more. Remove the toothpicks and watch as the carrots curl.

Growing Carrot Tops

You can grow a leafy plant from a carrot top. But since carrots grow underground from seeds, this plant will not grow a carrot to eat. You can also try this with the tops of beets, turnips, and parsnips. See how the leaves are different.

1. Cut a ½-inch thick slice from the top of a carrot.

2. Wet a paper towel with water. Lay it in the bottom of a plastic container.

3. Place the cut side of the carrot on the wet paper.

4. Put the container near a sunny window. Give it a little water every day or so to keep the paper wet. Leaves should begin to grow in about a week.

Read On

THE CARROT SEED
by Ruth Krauss

(Scholastic)

Beginning readers will love this classic story of a boy who plants a carrot seed and patiently waits for it to grow.

Beyond D

ABOUT

Dates go back over 5,000 years. Dates grow on giant date palm trees in warm, dry places. This is why they are called a desert fruit. The first dates came from India, but today they are also found in the Middle East and Africa. In the United States, they grow in California and Arizona. Dates are usually picked when they are hard and green. Then they are ripened off the tree. When ripe, most dates are dried, since food that is dried keeps for a long time. In the market, choose dried dates that are soft and plump, with smooth, shiny skin. Keep them in a closed container in a cool, dry place or in the refrigerator.

Orange Date Muffins

This makes 9 muffins. Enough for friends and family.

1½ cups whole wheat flour
½ cup wheat germ
2 teaspoons baking powder
½ teaspoon baking soda
½ teaspoon salt
1 teaspoon cinnamon
½ cup chopped dates
4 juice oranges
2 tablespoons oil

1. Set the oven to 375°F. and let it warm up.

2. Place paper liners in 9 of the spaces in a muffin pan.

3. In a large bowl, mix together the flour, wheat germ, baking powder, baking soda, salt, and cinnamon. Stir in the dates.

4. Squeeze the oranges to make 1¼ cups juice. Remove any pulp from inside the peel and add it to the juice.

5. Add the juice and the oil to the flour mixture. Stir gently, just until the dry ingredients are completely moistened.

6. Spoon the muffin batter into the muffin cups, so each one is a little more than half full.

7. Place the muffin pan in the oven and bake for 20 to 25 minutes, until the muffins are golden.

Creamy Date-Nut Spread

A spread for your bread.

farmer cheese or part skim milk ricotta cheese
chopped dates
chopped nuts.
pineapple juice
toast or muffins

1. Mash together farmer cheese or pot cheese, some chopped dates, and some chopped nuts.

2. Stir in pineapple juice, a spoonful at a time, until the mixture is creamy and easy to spread.

3. Spread on toast or muffins.

Don't eat too many. They are very sweet.

Recipes!

Dates Grow Here

THE MIDDLE EAST

THE UNITED STATES

NORTHERN AFRICA

The Joke Bag

Q: Why did the banana go out with the prune?

A: Because it couldn't get a date.

www.datesaregreat.com
Website for date lovers.

Beyond E

ABOUT

Most people think that the eggplant is a vegetable. It's really a fruit! Eggplants were first grown in India. Today, many countries grow them and use them in popular dishes. Plump purple eggplants are the most common kind. You may also see some that are long and skinny, with skin that is white or with lavender or green stripes. In the market, choose firm, smooth-skinned eggplants. You can get them at any time of year. Don't forget: eggplants spoil quickly. Store them in a cool, dry place and eat within a day or two of purchase.

INDIA

ABOUT the E picture

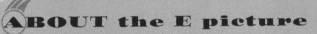

Although most eggplants are big and purple, some are small and white. It's easy to see why the hen is confused and how the eggplant got its name.

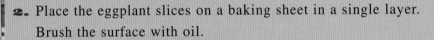

Recipe:
Purple Parmesan

Enough for 4 servings, so you can share it with 3 other people.

1 large eggplant (about 2 pounds)
olive oil
½ pound part skim milk mozzarella cheese
2 cups tomato sauce
¾ cup grated Parmesan cheese

1. Cut the eggplant into round slices about ¼ inch thick.

2. Place the eggplant slices on a baking sheet in a single layer. Brush the surface with oil.

3. Place the eggplant under the broiler and cook for about 5 minutes, until it is lightly browned. Using a spatula or a fork, turn the egg plant slices over. Brush them with oil. Return the pan to the broiler and cook for 3 minutes.

4. Cut the mozzarella cheese into thin slices.

5. Set the oven to 350°F. and let it warm up.

6. Cover the bottom of a 9 x 13-inch baking pan with a layer of the cooked eggplant. Cover the eggplant with a layer of sliced mozzarella cheese. Cover the cheese with a layer of tomato sauce. Sprinkle some of the grated cheese on top of the sauce. Repeat these layers until all of the eggplant is used up. Be sure to save some tomato sauce and Parmesan cheese to put on top at the end.

7. Place the baking pan in the oven. Bake for about 20 minutes, until the sauce bubbles and the cheese melts.

Campfire Packets

Here is a vegetable recipe you can cook outdoors on a barbecue grill or an open fire.

1 small eggplant
1 medium zucchini
1 tomato
1 green pepper
1 small onion
pepper
dried oregano
soy sauce
fresh lemon juice

1. Cut the eggplant, zucchini, and tomato into small chunks. Cut the green pepper into strips. Cut the onion into rings.

2. Cut heavy-duty aluminum foil into 4 squares, each about 12 inches. If you only have regular aluminum foil make it double thick.

3. Place an equal amount of each vegetable in the center of each aluminum foil square. Fold up the edges of the foil to make a bowl around the vegetables.

4. Season each packet of vegetables with some pepper, oregano, a few dashes of soy sauce, and a squirt of fresh lemon juice.

5. Fold the foil so the vegetables are all tucked inside. Fold the edges several times so the packets are well sealed.

6. Place the vegetable packets right in the hot coals of a barbecue grill or open fire. Cook for 20 minutes.

7. Using long tongs, carefully remove one packet of vegetables from the hot coals. Open it up and test the vegetables to see if they are done. They should be tender and a little charred. If they are not ready, close the packet. Put it back in the coals for 5 or 10 minutes. If they are done, take the other packets out.

8. Give each person a packet of vegetables. You can eat right out of the foil or put the vegetables on a plate. Be sure to let the vegetables cool a little before tasting, since they will be very hot.

Read On

STILL LIFE STEW
by Helena Clare Pittman
(Hyperion Books for Children)

We know young readers will like this book of colors, sizes, and shapes that inspire a girl's painting and a recipe for vegetable stew.

Beyond F

ABOUT

Farmers are the people whose job it is to grow food and other things we need, like cotton for clothing. Since we cannot live without food, farming may be the most important work on earth. Farms can be big or small. Some farms are called family farms because the families that take care of them also live there. Other farms are very big, and the workers live someplace else. These are called factory farms. Farmers have to be very patient, since many things take months or even years before they are ready to eat. Farming can be fun, too, since everyone on the farm gets to see the crops and animals grow. Farmers also feel good about feeding people. The next time you go to the market you should think of where all that food comes from. Don't forget – the farmer feeds us all.

ABOUT the F picture

This hardworking farmer sure looks familiar. Maybe next time, the reindeer will do some pulling!

Recipe: Farmer's Breakfast

Farmers eat hearty breakfasts. This one will feed 4 to 6 people, depending on how hungry the farmers – young and old – are.

3 large potatoes
1 large onion
½ green pepper
8 eggs
oil
salt, pepper

1. Cut the potatoes into chunks and boil them for about 15 minutes, until just tender.

2. Cut the cooked potatoes into thin slices. Cut the onion into thin slices. Chop the green pepper.

3. Crack the eggs into a bowl. Using a fork, beat the eggs until the yolks and whites are mixed together.

4. Heat enough oil to cover the surface of a large frying pan.

5. Put the onions in the pan and cook them until they get soft.

6. Add the potatoes to the pan and continue to cook everything over medium heat so the potatoes brown slowly. This will take about 25 minutes.

7. Add the green pepper to the pan. Add salt and pepper.

8. Turn the heat low. Pour the eggs over the vegetables. While the eggs cook, mix them with a large spoon until they aren't runny anymore.

You can be a farmer now

If you don't have a growing area where you live, don't worry. You can grow such vegetables as tomatoes and peppers in pots. Another good idea is to share a garden at a friend's house. Then you can share the work, the fun, and the harvest! Many places have community gardens where people garden together. You can learn about these neighborhood gardens from the American Community Garden Association, c/o Franklin Park Conservatory, 1777 East Broad Street, Columbus, OH 43203, www.communitygarden.org. The Landis Valley Museum is a museum of farming that you can visit online or in person. They also have a catalog of heirloom seeds. Heirloom Seed Project, 2451 Kissel Hill Rd., Lancaster, PA, 17601. www.landisvalleymuseum.org

Watch this

In the video "Fresh from the Family Farm," you can go with Nick and his mother on a visit to a family farm.

Available from Farm Aid, 11 Ward St., Ste. 200, Somerville, MA 02143. www.farmaid.org

Want to visit a farm?

Are there any farms nearby? If you or your class want to visit a farm, contact Agriculture in the Classroom, 1400 Independence Ave., Washington, DC 20250. www.agclassroom.org

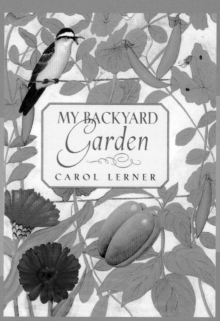

The Joke Bag

Q: Why can't clumsy farmers ever keep a secret?

A: They spill the beans.

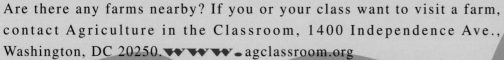

Read On

MY BACKYARD GARDEN
by Carol Lerner

(Morrow Junior Books)

An easy-to-follow guide to planting a vegetable garden.

G

Grapes have been around for 6,000 years. They were probably first grown by the Egyptians. They hang in bunches on small shrubs and climbing vines. Grapes are grown on most continents. Most of the grapes in the U.S. come from California, New York, and Michigan. There are thousands of grape varieties, but only a few are grown to be sold. Some grapes have several seeds in the center, while others are seedless. Grapes are divided into two types. Oddly, the ones called either black or red can range in color from light red to purple-black. Just as strange, the white group includes grapes that are yellow-green to light green. In the market, buy grapes that are plump, well colored and attached to their stems. Store them in a bowl in the refrigerator.

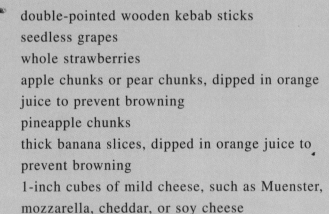

Counting Kebabs

A meal you can count on.

double-pointed wooden kebab sticks

seedless grapes

whole strawberries

apple chunks or pear chunks, dipped in orange juice to prevent browning

pineapple chunks

thick banana slices, dipped in orange juice to prevent browning

1-inch cubes of mild cheese, such as Muenster, mozzarella, cheddar, or soy cheese

1. Count how many kebab sticks you have.

2. Count how many pieces of each fruit you have.

3. Count how many cubes of cheese you have.

4. Make a pile of fruit and cheese in front of each kebab stick with the same amount of food in each pile.

5. Arrange the pieces of fruit and cheese in a colorful way on the kebab sticks.

Recipes

Great Frozen Grapes

A very cool snack.

seedless green grapes

1. Wash the grapes, remove them from the stem, and lay them in a metal pan in a single layer.

2. Place the pan of grapes in the freezer.

3. In a few hours, when the grapes are frozen, take them out of the pan and put them into a freezer container or plastic bag. Put them back in the freezer. Now, whenever you need a snack, you have a storehouse of great frozen grapes on hand.

How do you like these raisins?

You can make raisins! Start with a bunch of seedless grapes. Wash them in cold water and remove any that are bruised. Take the grapes off the stems and put them in a strainer. Dip the strainer into a pot of boiling water so the skins break. Remove the grapes from the boiling water and put them on a drying screen. You can make a drying screen by spreading clean cheesecloth, screening, or wire mesh over old picture frames or kitchen cooling racks. Spread the grapes out, so they don't touch each other. Depending on how many grapes there are, you may need more than one drying screen. Here are two ways you can dry the grapes. The first is to place the trays beside a sunny window for 4 to 5 days, turning them every few hours so the fruit dries evenly. The second way is to put the trays in a warm (140°F.) oven and let them stay there overnight. The grapes become raisins when they are at the dry, chewy stage.

Grapes Grow Here

ASIA

AUSTRALIA

EUROPE

USA

SOUTH AMERICA

True Food Fact

Raisins are dried grapes.
Other fruits that are dried are dates, prunes, figs, apples, apricots, peaches, pears, cranberries, papayas, mangoes, and pineapples. Dried food lasts longer. Want to make your own raisins? Take a look at

How do you like these raisins?

Tongue Twister

Say this five times fast:

green
grapes
grow
great

Grape
Mario Scalet

Stopwatch books

Read On

GRAPE
by Mario Scalet
(Stopwatch Books, Simon & Shuster)
You can see grapes grow from seed to harvest in this book's wonderful photos.

The Joke Bag

Q: What's green, big, and swims in the ocean?

A: Moby grape.

Q: Who is purple and your grandmother's brother?

A: Your grape-uncle.

Beyond

ABOUT Herbs are edible leaves and stems of plants that have special flavors and smells. Most people like herbs because they make food taste better. Some are also used as medicine. Cooks love herbs because they let them be creative with food. Sometimes the name of a food tells you what herb has been added – for example, dill pickles and mint tea. Most herbs are sold dried, but many can be found fresh, as well. In the market, choose herbs that have a nice fresh smell and a bright color, without any wilting or browning. To store them in the refrigerator, wrap them in a slightly damp paper towel inside a closed plastic bag. Store dried herbs in tightly closed containers in a cool, dry place in the kitchen. For best flavor try to use them up within 3 to 6 months.

Recipes

The special flavor in these recipes comes from the herbs. Make sure you taste and smell each herb.

Quick Dill Pickles

Quick to make – and quick to disappear!

2 unwaxed cucumbers
1 small onion
1 small clove garlic, chopped
1 tablespoon fresh dill
1 cup hot water
1 tablespoon salt
2 tablespoons honey
3 tablespoons white or cider vinegar

1. Slice each cucumber lengthwise into 8 sticks. Slice the onion into rings.

2. Layer the cucumber sticks and onion rings in a wide, nonmetal covered dish.

3. Scatter the dill and garlic on top.

4. Mix the hot water with the salt and honey to dissolve. Add the vinegar. Pour this mixture over the cucumbers. Cover and refrigerate for at least 6 hours before using. You can keep these Quick Pickles in the refrigerator for several weeks.

Guacamole Dip

Guacamole is a Mexican dip. It is made with an herb called cilantro. Scoop it up with chips or vegetables or for a treat, try jicama slices (see the letter J).

1 clove garlic
1 large ripe Haas or California avocado
1 tablespoon lemon juice
1 small tomato, chopped
$\frac{1}{2}$ teaspoon salt
$\frac{1}{4}$ teaspoon hot pepper sauce or to taste
2 tablespoons chopped fresh cilantro

1. Cut the garlic clove in half and rub a bowl well with the cut surface.

2. Cut the avocado in half. Remove the pit and scoop out the "meat." Put it in the bowl rubbed with garlic. Mash it with a fork or potato masher.

3. Add the lemon juice, tomato, salt, and hot pepper sauce. Mix well.

4. Sprinkle the cilantro on top.

Drinking Herbs

Herbs make great tea. You can drink them hot or cold. Two popular types are mint and chamomile. You can make these and other herb teas using tea bags from the store. You can also make tea from the fresh herb itself - for example, mint, which is easy to grow.

Mint Tea

1 tablespoon fresh mint leaves or 1 teaspoon dried mint

1 cup boiling water

1. Put the mint in a tea strainer and place the strainer in a mug.

2. Pour boiling water into the mug. Let it sit for 3 minutes.

3. Remove the tea strainer. Sweeten with a little honey, if you like. When the tea is cool enough, drink it.

Herbs put on a plate to make the food look prettier are called a garnish.

One familiar garnish is parsley. If you have parsley on your plate, don't forget to eat it. Parsley has a nice taste, is good for you, and makes your breath sweet.

The Joke Bag

Q: What's green and sings?

A: Elvis Parsley.

Be an herb gardener

Herbs are easy to grow. They don't need much room, they are nice to look at, and you can cook with them. You can get herb seeds in a garden shop or from a seed catalog such as Seed Savers Exchange/ Flower & Herb Exchange, 3094 N. Winn Rd., Decorah, IA 52101 **www.**seedsaversexchange.org

Herb Cards

How about greeting cards that smell like your favorite herb? What you need:

dried herbs of your choice, such as chamomile, dill, fennel, lavender, marjoram, rosemary, thyme
heavy paper
clear laminating paper
scissors
pen

1. Cut the paper so it is two times the size of the card you want to make. Fold in half. Cut a piece of clear laminating paper the same size as the finished card.

2. Place the herb in the center of the right half of the paper.

3. Place the laminating paper over the right half of the paper. Rub the laminating paper to seal in the herb.

4. Fold the card with the herb on the outside. Write your message inside.

Beyond I

ABOUT the I poem

The answer is "yes." To find out why read **ABOUT** on this page.

ABOUT Indians in the mountains of Peru and Bolivia began growing potatoes more than 7,000 years ago. Now they are grown in more that 150 countries. Even though there are hundreds of kinds of potatoes, only a few are sold in grocery stores. The potato called the Idaho was first grown by Luther Burbank, who lived in the state of Idaho. This potato is also called a Burbank and a russet. No matter where this potato is grown, it can be called an Idaho. In the market, look for firm potatoes with a nice shape and no bad spots. Do not eat potatoes if they have any sprouts or large areas of green under the skin. Store potatoes in a cool, dark, airy place for up to 2 weeks.

How do you like these potatoes?

Potatoes come in many shapes, sizes, and colors. Small round potatoes that have just been picked are called new potatoes. Their thin skin may be tan or red. Large, mature potatoes such as Idahos are a darker brown and have thicker skins. The potato that is called Yukon gold has a slightly sweet flavor and a smooth buttery texture. Some markets sell potatoes that are no bigger than your finger. There are even potatoes that are purple both inside and out. How many have you tasted?

A HOT POTATO is something you don't want to touch – a problem

A COUCH POTATO is a lazy person

Recipes!

Smashed Spud Soup

Spud is another name for potato. This recipe is enough for 4 for on a cold winter day.

1 pound potatoes
1½ cups water
3½ cups lowfat milk
2 teaspoons grated onion
¼ cup natural peanut butter
1 tablespoon butter
¼ cup ketchup
salt
pepper

1. Peel the potatoes and cut them into one-inch pieces.

2. Add the potatoes to the water in a pot. Bring to a boil, cover, and cook for 15 to 20 minutes, until the potatoes are very soft.

3. Mash the potatoes in the pot with a potato masher, until they are completely smashed.

4. Stir the milk, onion, peanut butter, and butter into the potatoes. Cook over medium heat, stirring now and then, until the mixture starts to boil.

5. Cook the soup a little longer, until it is thick and creamy.

6. Stir in the ketchup. Add a little salt and pepper, until the soup tastes the way you like it.

Ida's Oven Fries

This is a better way to make "fried" potatoes. Enough for 4.

1 pound potatoes
1 tablespoon oil
½ teaspoon paprika

1. Set the oven to 450°F. and let it warm up.

2. Scrub the potatoes, but leave on the skins.

3. Cut the potatoes into sticks, as for French fries.

4. Combine the potatoes in a big bowl with the oil. Mix well, so the potatoes are all coated with oil. Add the paprika and mix again.

5. Dampen a paper towel with a little more oil. Use it to oil a cookie sheet or a large baking pan. Spread the potatoes in a single layer on the baking pan.

6. Bake the potatoes for 10 minutes. Use a spatula to carefully loosen the potatoes from the pan. Shake the pan gently to keep the potatoes from sticking.

7. Bake the potatoes for 20 to 30 minutes more. When they are done the outside will be firm but the inside will be soft. Shake the pan a few times during cooking so the potatoes stay loose. Be sure to protect your hand with a pot holder or oven mitt.

▼▼▼▼▼ potatomuseum.com
Visit the Potato Museum for all things potato.

Potato Stamps

You can make pictures with potatoes! You will need a big potato, a knife, a marker, poster paint, and paper. Cut the potato in half with a sharp knife. Use a marker to draw a simple design on the cut surface of the potato. Cut away the potato from around the design. Pour some liquid poster paint into a shallow disposable dish. Dip the cut side of the potato into the paint. Press this onto a piece of paper. Gently lift the potato to see your print. Do it again and again, and you will make a pattern.

Stopwatch books
Potato
Barrie Watts

Read On

POTATO
by Barrie Watts.

(Stopwatch Books, Silver Burdett Press)

How potatoes grow. Terrific color photos.

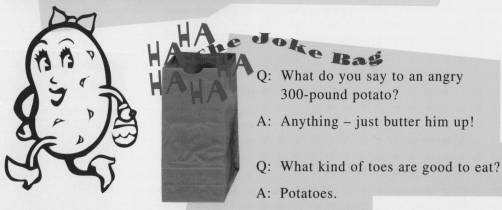

The Joke Bag

Q: What do you say to an angry 300-pound potato?

A: Anything – just butter him up!

Q: What kind of toes are good to eat?

A: Potatoes.

Beyond J

ABOUT The jicama (HEE-ca-ma) is a root vegetable, just like the carrot and the radish. It is big and round and white under its thin brown skin, and looks like a potato. Jicama doesn't taste like a potato, though. It is crisp and sweet, and you can eat it either raw or cooked. In Mexico, where jicama comes from, people peel and slice it for a snack. Jicama isn't sold everywhere, but you can find it in many supermarkets or small markets where Spanish-speaking people shop. You can also find it in Oriental markets, where it goes by the name yam bean.

Recipes:

Jicama Dip-ama

Dip sliced jicama into salsa. It's better than chips! This is a very mild salsa. For a spicy salsa, add hot pepper sauce.

- 1 jicama, a little bigger than a softball
- 3 tablespoons fresh lime juice
- 2 large ripe tomatoes
- 2 scallions, thinly sliced
- 1 clove garlic, chopped
- 2 tablespoons chopped fresh cilantro *or*
- flat-leaf parsley plus ½ teaspoon cumin

1. Using a small, sharp knife, remove the brown skin from the jicama.

2. Cut the jicama into thin round slices or 2-inch long sticks. Place them in a bowl. Stir in 1 tablespoon of the lime juice.

3. To make the salsa, chop the tomatoes. Put them in a serving bowl along with any juice that leaked out while you were chopping.

4. Add the remaining 2 tablespoons of the lime juice and the seasonings to the tomatoes. Mix well.

5. Put the jicama on a plate next to the bowl of salsa. Dip a piece of jicama into the salsa, eat it, and shout, "Olé!"

With a favorite dip or plain.

Mexican Confetti

Here is a vegetable side dish for 4 grownups or 6 to 8 kids.

- 1 jicama, about the size of a softball
- 1 sweet red or green pepper
- 1 small onion
- 2 cloves garlic
- 1 tablespoon olive oil
- 1 cup fresh or frozen corn kernels
- salt, pepper

1. Using a small sharp knife, remove the brown skin from the jicama.

2. Cut the jicama, sweet pepper, and onion into bite-size pieces. Chop the garlic or squeeze it in a garlic press.

3. Heat the oil in a large skillet. When it is hot, add all the vegetables. Cook over medium-high heat. Stir every few minutes, so the vegetables cook and don't stick to the pan.

4. Cook for about 10 minutes, until the vegetables are tender but still crunchy. If you want the vegetables softer, cook them longer.

5. Add salt and pepper to taste.

ABOUT the J poem

Spanish is a language spoken in many parts of the world. When you say the word Spanish you are using an English word. (You are reading English right now.) This may sound funny, but the word Español (Es-Pan-YOL) in the poem is the Spanish word for "Spanish." Different languages pronounce letters differently from English. As the poem says, in Spanish J can be pronounced like an H. Here are some other Spanish words that start with a J but sound like H: José (Joe), Julio (July), Junio (June), joyas (jewelry), jugo (juice).

Jicama grows here

MEXICO

Spanish spoken here:

SPAIN

MEXICO

CENTRAL AMERICA

SOUTH AMERICA

Some other Mexican foods

chilies, corn, papaya, avocado, tomatillos, nopale cactus

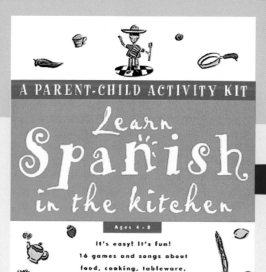

A PARENT-CHILD ACTIVITY KIT

Learn **Spanish** in the kitchen

Ages 4-8

It's easy! It's fun!
16 games and songs about food, cooking, tableware, and cleaning up!

48-PAGE BOOK WITH STICKERS

60-MINUTE CASSETTE

LIVING LANGUAGE®
A Random House Company

Read On

LEARN SPANISH IN THE KITCHEN
by Gretchen Patterson

(Living Language Parent/Child Activity Kit)

Learn some Spanish and about cooking, too.

Beyond K

ABOUT The kiwi fruit was first grown in China, where it was called Chinese gooseberry. The name kiwi comes from a little brown bird that lives in New Zealand. The fruit was given the new name kiwi, because New Zealand is where most kiwi fruit now comes from. Kiwis also grow in California. The kiwi fruit looks like a large egg covered with fuzzy brown hair. Inside it is usually a bright, beautiful green, with tiny black seeds that you can eat. It tastes like a delicious mix of pineapple and strawberry. Kiwis are available all year. Ripe kiwis can be stored in the refrigerator up to 3 weeks.

Kiwis grow here

OOH!

Kiwis can be cut in half and scooped out with a spoon.

NEW ZEALAND

ASIA

Recipe:

Kiwi Pie

This pie will feed 8 to 10 people. Keep in mind that one of the ingredients, yogurt cheese, takes a day to make – so plan in advance.

Crust:

1 1/4 cups crumbs made from plain or chocolate graham crackers
1/4 cup wheat germ
2 to 4 tablespoons orange juice

Filling:

2 tablespoons honey
1 teaspoon vanilla extract
1 1/2 cups yogurt cheese

Yogurt cheese is easy to make. Gravity does all the work! Just line a mesh strainer with cheesecloth, a drip coffee filter or use a special yogurt cheese maker. Set this on a bowl. Pour in at least 3 cups of plain yogurt. Put it in the refrigerator for 24 hours. The soft cheese that remains in the strainer is yogurt cheese.

Topping:

3 cups sliced peeled kiwi
2 tablespoons honey
1 tablespoon cornstarch
2 tablespoons lemon juice

1. Set the oven to 350°F. and let it warm up.

2. Make the crumbs for the crust by putting the cookies in a plastic bag and crushing them with a rolling pin, or by grinding the cookies in a blender or food processor.

3. Combine the cookies and the wheat germ in a bowl. Add just enough juice so the mixture holds together when you press it between your fingers.

4. Put the crumbs in a 9-inch pie pan. Use your hand to press them down, so they completely cover the bottom and sides of the pan.

5. Bake the crust for 8 minutes. Take it out of the oven and let it cool.

6. To make the filling, use a fork to beat the honey and vanilla into the yogurt cheese. Refrigerate the filling if it isn't used right away. When the crust is at room temperature, fill it with the sweetened yogurt cheese.

7. To make the topping, put 1 cup of the kiwi slices in a small pot. Mash them with a fork or potato masher. Add the honey, cornstarch, and lemon juice. Set the pot over low heat. Cook, stirring all the time, until the mixture is thick and clear and no longer has a milky look. Remove the pot from the heat. Let the cooked kiwi cool for a few minutes.

8. Use the remaining 2 cups of kiwi slices to cover the filling.

9. Using a spoon, gently spread the cooked kiwi over the top of the pie, until the fruit is completely covered. This layer is called a "glaze."

10. Leave the pie in the refrigerator for a few hours before serving.

Kookie Game

If you didn't know kiwi is a fruit, what would you think it is? Can you make up other funny-sounding fruit names starting with K?

Here are some: Kibbika, Kookoola, Klushpot.

Other fruits that come from:

New Zealand

Braeburn apple
Fuji apple
Granny Smith apple
Royal Gala apple
passion fruit
pepino
tamarillo

China

kumquats
jujubes
loquats
lychees
winter melons

Beyond L

ABOUT The first lemons grew wild in China, Myanmar (Burma), and India. Christopher Columbus brought the lemon across the Atlantic Ocean to North America. In the United States today, most lemons are grown in California, Arizona, and Florida. Lemons belong to a family of fruit called citrus. Limes, oranges, tangerines, and grapefruits are all citrus fruits. In the market, choose lemons that are firm and bright yellow. They can be kept in the refrigerator for 2 to 3 weeks.

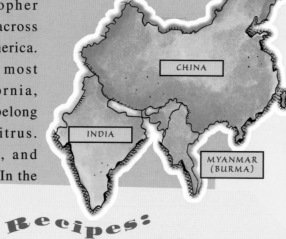

CHINA

INDIA

MYANMAR (BURMA)

Recipes:

Real Fresh Lemonade

Makes 1 quart or 4 tall glasses of refreshing lemonade.

3 lemons
3 tablespoons honey
1 cup hot water
2 cups cold water

1. Squeeze the lemons to make ½ cup lemon juice.

2. In a 1-quart jar, stir the honey into the hot water until it melts.

3. Add the lemon juice and cold water to the honey-water.

4. Put the lemonade into the refrigerator until it is cold.

Greek Coleslaw

In Greece, people make coleslaw by mixing fresh lemon juice into cabbage with their hands. This recipe will feed four to six people. (Make sure to wash your hands well.)

4 cups coarsely shredded cabbage
juice of ½ lemon

1. Fill a big bowl with the shredded cabbage. Use your hands to squeeze the cabbage until it softens.

2. Squeeze in the lemon juice and mix it with the cabbage.

Lemon Squash and Carrots

The whole lemon, including the peel, is used to flavor carrots and the yellow squash called crookneck. Use an organic lemon if you can. Enough for six people.

1½ cups peeled, thinly sliced carrots
2 cups thinly sliced crookneck squash
1 small whole lemon, thinly sliced
1 tablespoon honey
½ cup water
¼ teaspoon cinnamon

1. Combine all the ingredients in a saucepan and bring to a boil.

2. Cover and cook gently over low heat for about 8 minutes, until the carrots are just tender.

How Do You Like These Lemons?

Lemon juice and lemon peel are used in cooking to wake up other foods' flavors. Try squeezing a little fresh lemon juice on vegetable salads, fruit salads, or cooked vegetables. Can you taste the difference?

Lemon Juice Cleans

If your hands are smelly, wipe them with lemon peel and see how nice they smell. Here is a recipe for making furniture polish using lemon juice.

¼ cup vegetable oil
¼ cup lemon juice

1. Put the ingredients in a small glass jar. Shake well.

2. Using an all-cotton cloth, wipe a little of the mixture on furniture until it is shiny.

HERE'S A LEMON YOU CAN'T EAT!

Sometimes you hear someone say that their car is a LEMON

What they mean is that the car keeps breaking down. This is because another meaning for this word is "no good."

True Food Fact

To get the most juice from a lemon, let it come to room temperature. Then roll it on the counter, before you cut and squeeze it.

Grow Your Own Lemon Plant

You can grow lemon plants from lemon seeds. Give your little "lemon trees" to friends. All you need is a 4-inch flowerpot, some potting soil, and a few lemon seeds.

1. Choose seeds that are plump. Wash and dry them.

2. Fill the flower pot with soil. Place several lemon seeds 1 inch apart on the soil.

3. Cover the seeds with ¼-inch of soil. Pat down gently. Water, cover with a plastic bag, and place near a sunny window.

4. When the plant appears, remove the bag. Continue to water every few days, as needed. Don't let the soil dry out. Watch for signs of the growing plant. It can take from 3 weeks to 3 months.

Lemon Magic

To write a secret message or draw an invisible picture, dip a fine paint brush or cotton swab in lemon juice. Use this as your "ink." When it dries it will be invisible. To see what you have written or drawn, warm the paper over a light bulb. The secret will be revealed.

the Joke Bag

Customer: " Waiter, there's a fly in my lemonade! What is it doing there?"

Waiter: " It looks like the dog paddle."

HA HA HA HA HA HA HA HA HA

Beyond M

ABOUT

The first mangoes came from India. Today they are grown in warm places around the world – including Haiti, Mexico, California, and Florida. Because of their juiciness and unusual sweet and tart taste, mangoes are sometimes called the "peach of the tropics." Mangoes are found in stores all year long. In the market, look for slightly firm fruit, showing some yellow or red on the green skin. Use your nose – the fruit should have a flowery smell. Mangoes that are hard can be ripened in a paper bag at room temperature. They are ready to eat when they are not green anymore and they feel a little soft when you press them gently with your fingers. Ripe mangoes can be kept in the refrigerator for up to 5 days.

Don't forget
the lime!

ABOUT the M poem

The original Mayans who you see in the picture really didn't do the tango – but we love the silly rhyme. The original Mayans were a people who lived in Central America more than 1,000 years ago. This was long before the tango was invented. The Mayans were amazing. They developed math, and the calendar, and built beautiful buildings. If you go to countries like Mexico and Guatemala, you can still see the large Mayan pyramids that are in the picture. You can also meet the descendants of the original Mayans. The poem is right about one thing – a little fresh lime makes mango taste even better.

Recipe:

Mango Tango Jam

Use this like any other jam, or eat it the way they do in South America. There they spread it on crackers and put a slice of mild white cheese on top. In Spanish, this cheese is called "queso blanco," (kay-so blank-o) or white cheese. If you can't find it, you can use mozzarella cheese. This recipe makes about 1½ cups of jam and will keep for several weeks in the refrigerator.

2 ripe mangoes
½ lemon
¼ cup honey
½ cup water

1. Peel the mangoes with a small, sharp knife. Slice the meat from the pit.

2. Squeeze the lemon into a small pot. Chop some of the lemon peel into tiny pieces and add it to the pot.

3. Add the honey and the water to the lemon juice. Set the pot on the stove over medium heat. Bring the liquid to a boil.

4. Add the mango slices to the pot. Cook over low heat. When the fruit starts to get soft, mash it gently with a potato masher or a fork. Cook for about 20 minutes, until the jam is thick.

5. Spoon the jam into a jar. Put it into the refrigerator until it is very cold.

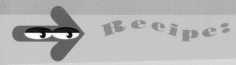

Creamy Mango Salad Dressing

1 mango
1 lime wedge
¼ cup plain, lowfat yogurt
water

1. Peel the mango with a small, sharp knife. Slice the meat from the pit.

2. Put the mango slices in a blender or food processor. Squeeze the lime wedge onto the mango. Turn on the machine and let it run until the fruit is smooth.

3. Spoon the mango into a bowl. Stir in the yogurt. Add as much water as you need to make a creamy dressing. Pour the dressing over your favorite fruit or green salad.

Mangos Grow Here

MEXICO

HAITI

Read On

THE MARKET LADY AND THE MANGO TREE
by Pete and Mary Watson.

(Tambourine Books)

A story for new readers about West African children and a woman who discovers that no good comes from trying to trick people.

The Joke Bag

HA HA HA HA HA HA HA HA

Here's the weather forecast from Mexico:

Chile today.
Hot tamale.

www.freshmangos.com
Mango history, facts, myths and more.

Learn how to peel and slice a mango at
www.lancaster.unl.edu/food/ciq-mango.htm

Beyond N

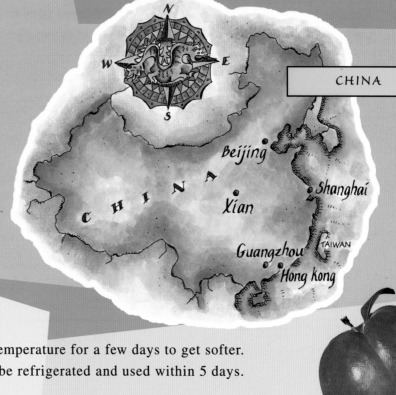

CHINA

ABOUT The nectarine is like a peach with no fuzz! It got its start in China about 2,000 years ago. Nectarines can be used just like peaches in fruit desserts. You will find nectarines at the store from mid spring to late September, but they are best during July and August. In the market, look for sweet smelling, brightly colored fruit. Squeeze gently to see if it is ready to eat. It should feel a little soft. If you buy nectarines that are still hard, leave them at room temperature for a few days to get softer. Nectarines that are ready to eat should be refrigerated and used within 5 days.

GO...

Eat a nectarine and a peach. Which one do you like better?

Recipe:

Nectarine Nectar

1/3 cup cut-up nectarines
1/3 cup fresh or frozen raspberries
1/3 cup orange juice

1. Put the fruit and juice in a blender. Run the machine until the fruit is smooth.

2. Pour the juice into a tall glass and drink it.

Recipe: Fresh Nectarine Cake

This cake is a little bit of work – but worth it!

1 egg

¼ cup honey

pinch of salt

½ cup plain, lowfat yogurt

½ teaspoon almond extract

1 cup whole wheat flour

½ teaspoon baking soda

2 cups sliced fresh nectarines

2 tablespoons maple syrup

¼ teaspoon cinnamon

1. Set the oven to 375°F. and let it warm up.

2. In a large bowl, beat the egg with the honey. Beat in the salt, yogurt, and almond extract until the mixture is smooth.

3. In a separate bowl, mix the flour with the baking soda. Gently stir the flour into the egg-and-yogurt until it is well mixed. The batter is ready when you can't see any dry flour.

4. Wet a paper towel with oil and wipe the inside of an 8-inch square baking pan until it is coated with oil.

5. Pour the cake batter into the baking pan. Place the nectarine slices close together all over the top of the batter. Using a spoon, pour the maple syrup evenly over the fruit. Sprinkle the cinnamon evenly on top.

6. Place the cake in the oven for 30 minutes, or until it is baked in the middle. To see if it is done, insert a toothpick in the center. If it comes out clean the cake is ready. If the toothpick is covered with batter, the cake needs to stay in the oven for a few more minutes.

How To Ripen Fruit

Often the fruit you buy at the market isn't ripe. This means it hasn't reached its best flavor yet. There is something you can do about this. Here is an experiment you can try to decide if it works:

Take two hard unripe nectarines. Put one in the refrigerator. Put the other one in a small brown paper bag. Close the bag completely and let it sit for a day or two on the kitchen counter. Taste both nectarines. Which one is sweeter?

The Joke Bag

Knock, knock. Who's there? Nectarine. Nectarine who?

Knock, knock. Who's there? Nectarine. Nectarine who?

Knock, knock. Who's there? Nectarine. Nectarine who?

Knock, knock. Who's there? Orange. Orange who?

Orange you glad I didn't say Nectarine!

www.freshforkids.com/nec_index.htm
All about nectarines.

Beyond

ABOUT Organic food is grown in a way that is friendly to nature. A lot of food is grown with harmful chemicals. Not all chemicals are bad, but many of them are not good for the air, water, animals, farmers, or the people who eat the food. Organic farms don't use these chemicals. Organic farmers use farm wastes such as corn stalks, leaves and animal manure to help plants grow. These materials break down and feed the soil. Organic farmers are clever. For example, they keep insects from eating their crops with other bugs, like wasps and ladybugs, that eat the pesky insects. They stop weeds from growing by putting a blanket of plant waste called mulch around their crops. They also use machines to remove weeds.

These types of labels tell you a food is organic:

Recipes:

Your Own Organic Salad Bar

Why not set up a salad bar at home for family and friends? Start by choosing organic foods that you like. Now put on your chef's apron. Clean and cut your selections into bite-size pieces. Display them on platters or in bowls with serving utensils. Include salad dressing, whole wheat bread or crackers, too. Place everything on the kitchen counter or a table. Give each person a plate and have a feast.

    mixed leafy greens, such as leaf lettuce, romaine, spinach, mesclun
    bite-size pieces of raw broccoli, cauliflower, green beans, cucumber, zucchini, avocado, radish, tomato,
        mushrooms, jicama, carrots, beets, green peas
    bite-size pieces of any leftover cooked vegetables, such as potato, corn or any of the vegetables above
    bite-size pieces of fruit such as apples, pears, melon, orange wedges, grapes
    cooked beans, such as chickpeas, kidney beans, navy beans, lentils
    toasted pumpkin seeds or sunflower seeds
    bite-size cubes of tofu
    bite-size cubes of cheese
    favorite salad dressings

Shopping for Organic Food

Who sells organic food in your neighborhood? Organic fruits and vegetables can often be found at farm stands, natural food stores, and even in many supermarkets.

Organic Food by Mail

If there is no good place to get organic food where you live, you can get it by mail. Here is a great place to find more organic food sources.

www.organic-growers.com

The Joke Bag

HA HA HA HA HA HA

Q: Why shouldn't you tell secrets in the garden?

A: Because corn has ears and potatoes have eyes.

Friendly Trick

Say to your friends, "I am about to show you something that you have never seen before and you will never see again." Take out a piece of organic fruit or vegetable and show it to them. Then ask them "Have you ever seen this before?" When they say, "No," you say, "And you will never see it again," and pop it in your mouth. (Make sure you have some more to share with them.)

Read On

BLUE POTATOES, ORANGE TOMATOES
by Rosalind Creasy
(Sierra Club Books)

If you are a good reader, take a look at this book about growing vegetables in weird colors.

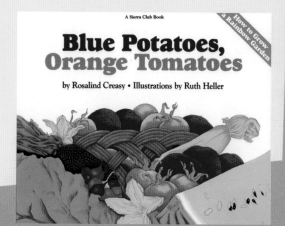

A Sierra Club Book

How to Grow a Rainbow Garden

Blue Potatoes, Orange Tomatoes
by Rosalind Creasy • Illustrations by Ruth Heller

Beyond P

At one time peas were rare–only rich people could afford them. But now they are available everywhere. These treats grow in pods and are also known as green peas and sugar peas. Pods are like little packages. To eat the peas, you must open the pods. How about eating the pods? You can with another kind of pea called a snow pea. Peas taste the sweetest just after they are picked, so you should eat them when they are very fresh. Peas aren't just for rich people anymore, but if you want them you have to be quick. They are in the store mostly in the late spring and early summer and again in the fall. In the market, choose fresh bright-green pods filled with lots of peas. You don't want peas that are flat or have soft, mushy spots. Refrigerate peas in their pods and try to eat them all in 2 to 3 days.

OOH!

Fresh Peas are a super snack.

Recipe:

The Captain's Split Pea Soup

When full grown, green peas are sometimes dried. Dried peas that have their skins removed are often split in two pieces. These "split peas" are famous for making soup. Here is a recipe that will feed 8.

2 cups dried split peas
8 cups water
2 onions
2 carrots
4 to 6 leafy celery tops
1 large bay leaf
2 teaspoons salt
pepper
whole wheat croutons or crackers

1. Combine the split peas and the water in a big soup pot. Bring to a boil.

2. While you are waiting for the water to boil, chop the onions and add them to the soup pot. Peel and chop the carrots and add them to the soup pot. Cut up the celery leaves and add them to the soup pot.

3. When the soup comes to a boil, add the bay leaf and salt. Cover the pot, turn the heat very low, and cook the soup for 1 to 1½ hours, until the peas are soft.

4. Mash the soup with a potato masher or the back of a wooden spoon or puree it in a food mill. Cook a few more minutes, with the cover off, to thicken the soup and get it nice and hot.

5. Ladle the soup into serving bowls. Grind some fresh pepper on top. Add a small handful of whole wheat croutons or crushed whole wheat crackers. Dig in.

The Joke Bag

Knock, knock.
Who's there?
Peas.
Peas who?
Peas open the door!

Q: What is green and flies?

A: Super pea.

PICKIN' PEAS

retold by
Margaret Read MacDonald

pictures by
Pat Cummings

Read On

When someone says
THEY ARE LIKE
TWO PEAS IN A POD
it means two people are
like each other

YOU KNOW YOUR
PEAS AND CARROTS
(p's and q's)
You are smart!

Sprouting Peas

Dried whole green peas make delicious sprouts. You can make them by following the directions on the "S" page.

PICKIN' PEAS
by Margaret Read MacDonald
(HarperCollins)

An old southern folktale for beginning readers.

Another Pea Poem

I eat my peas with honey,

I've done it all my life.

It may taste kind of funny,

But it keeps them on my knife.

Beyond Q

ABOUT

The quince is one of the world's oldest fruits. It grew in Iran more than 4,000 years ago. Today quince are grown in Turkey, South America, and all over the Mediterranean area. Quince has golden skin and looks like a combination of apple and pear. When ripe, it smells like perfume. But the flavor is tart, and it is always cooked before eating. Quince is very popular in jams and jellies. If you want to try one, you may have to wait. They are only available from October through December. In the market, select fruit that is large, yellow, and firm, with little or no green. If they are green, let them ripen at room temperature. Once ripe, they will keep in the refrigerator.

Quince Grow Here

TURKEY AND THE MEDITERRANIAN

Recipes: John Q's Baked Quince

1 medium quince per person
chopped walnuts or pecans
honey or maple syrup
apple juice

1. Set the oven to 375°F. and let it warm up.

2. Remove the core from each quince to within ½ inch of the bottom. Pack chopped nuts into the space where the core was. Pour in honey or maple syrup to cover the nuts.

3. Place the quince in a baking dish. Pour enough apple juice around the quince so that it is ½ inch deep.

4. Bake the quince for 30 minutes, until tender but not mushy. Stick a fork into the fruit to see if it is ready. If it isn't done, keep baking.

5. Serve the Baked Quince warm or chilled. If you like, you can put a spoonful of vanilla or lemon yogurt on top.

ABOUT the Q Picture

In this picture, we are having fun with the word quince. In our fantasy National Quince Museum, you see the fruit in make-believe paintings and sculpture, as well as a portrait of a real person, John Quincy Adams. John Quincy Adams was the sixth President of the United States. Not included in our "quince collection" is the town of Quincy, Massachusetts.

IRAN

SOUTH
AMERICA

TONGUE TWISTER
Say this four times fast:
The quince can't quite quit

True Food Fact

In the Portuguese language, the name for quince is "marmelo." This is where the word marmalade came from.

Read On

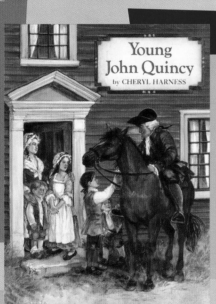

Young John Quincy by CHERYL HARNESS

Here is a book about President John Quincy Adams. We are not sure if he ate quince. We know he had an exciting life and did a lot of important things.

YOUNG JOHN QUINCY ADAMS

by Cheryl Harness

(Bradbury)

The early history of the United States through the eyes of young John Quincy Adams.

The Joke Bag

HA HA HA HA HA HA HA

Q: What do you have when 75 quince try to get through the same door?

A: Quince jam.

WWW.whitehouse.gov/history/presidents/ja6.html

The life of John Quincy Adams.

Q's You Can Use

There are no other common fruits or vegetables that begin with Q – so let's take a look at the letter Q. Here are some other words that begin with Q: quick, quack, quiet. And here is a vegetable with a Q in it: squash. Speaking of squash, how many of these kinds of squash have you tried? Acorn, butternut, crookneck, hubbard, zucchini.

Beyond R

ABOUT The radish is a root vegetable. Some other vegetables that grow underground which you may know are beets, carrots, and turnips. Radishes have been relished for more than 4,000 years. They come in an amazing assortment of colors, shapes, and sizes. Radishes can be red, white, purple, or black. Their shape can be round, oval, or long. The flavor of a radish can be mild to spicy. Small red radishes are the most common kind and are in stores all year long. They may come with their leaves and roots still on, or trimmed and packaged in plastic bags. In the market, select radishes that feel firm when gently squeezed. Remove any leaves and refrigerate the radishes in a plastic bag for up to 5 days.

Try a raw radish, but remember radishes are sometimes very spicy!

Recipes:

Russian Radish Salad

Enough for 4.

1 sprig fresh dill
2/3 cup thinly sliced red radishes
2/3 cup thinly sliced cucumber
2 scallions, thinly sliced
1/4 teaspoon salt
1/4 cup plain, lowfat yogurt

1. Using a kitchen scissors, snip the feathery part of the dill into tiny pieces. Throw away the stalk.

2. Mix all the ingredients together in a bowl.

3. Eat right away or place in the refrigerator for later.

Spunky Crunchy Spinach Salad

Serves 6.

Soy-Sesame Dressing:
- 1 tablespoon sesame seeds
- ¼ cup lemon juice
- 1 tablespoon soy sauce
- ¼ cup olive oil
- 1 tablespoon chopped sweet onion

1. Toast the sesame seeds in a small frying pan for about 1 minute. When you smell them toasting, but before they turn brown, remove the pan from the heat.

2. Combine the toasted sesame seeds with the lemon juice, soy sauce, oil, and onion in a jar. Cover the jar and shake the dressing.

Salad:
- 6 cups torn spinach leaves
- 2 cups sliced celery
- ¼ cup thinly sliced red or white radish

1. Put the spinach leaves in a salad bowl.

2. Arrange the celery and the radish slices on top of the spinach.

3. Just before you serve the salad, pour the dressing on top and mix it well.

True Food  Fact

Radishes can grow to 3 feet long and weigh 100 pounds.

Radish Ruse

(A ruse is a trick.)

Bend your elbow and balance a radish on the top of it. Now, lower your whole hand quickly so the radish drops off your elbow. If you do it fast enough, you will be able to catch the radish in your hand. Now take a nibble.

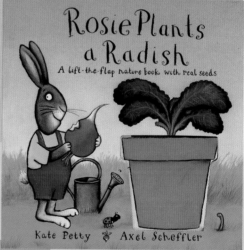

Read On

ROSIE PLANTS A RADISH

A Lift-The-Flap Nature Book With Real Seeds
by Kate Petty and Axel Scheffler

(Andrews McMeel Publishing)

Learn how plants grow by lifting the book's flaps to see what's happening underground.

Beyond S

ABOUT Sprouts are the tiny plants that you see when beans and seeds start to grow. You can buy sprouts at the store but it is easy to grow them yourself. Look on this page and see how. Some terrific sprouts are alfalfa, clover, and mung bean. The sprouts from peas, chickpeas, and radish and sunflower seeds taste just like these foods. If you are buying sprouts, choose crisp-looking sprouts with the seed still on them. Don't buy sprouts if any are dark or slimy-looking. Keep sprouts in the refrigerator in a container that allows some air. Eat them as soon as possible. Don't forget – you can be a sprout farmer and supply your family with fresh vegetables every day!

How to be a sprout farmer

Anyone can grow sprouts at home. You don't need a garden or soil. You hardly even need any space. The best spot is near a sink since you do need water. Sprouts can be grown from almost any kind of bean or special sprouting seed. Here are some suggestions: dried peas, chickpeas, lentils, soybeans, mung beans, kidney beans, alfalfa seeds, radish seeds, sunflower seeds, whole wheat or rye kernels. Wow – lots of choices! You can buy sprouting seeds at natural food stores or by mail. One good place is Sproutpeople, 170 Mendell St., San Francisco, CA 94124 www.sproutpeople.com.

Recipe: Chinese Chow Mein

In China, bean sprouts are very popular. The type of cooking used here, where vegetables are cooked quickly and mixed while cooking, is called "stir frying."

2 tablespoons oil

2 medium onions, cut into thin wedges

4 stalks celery, cut into ½-inch pieces

1 pound green beans, cut into 1-inch pieces

1½ cups water

2 teaspoons molasses

½ teaspoon salt

2 tablespoons soy sauce

3 cups bean sprouts

2/3 cup sliced almonds

2 teaspoons cornstarch

1. Heat oil in a wok or large skillet. Stir-fry the onion and celery together for 5 minutes.

2. Add the green beans and stir-fry 1 more minute.

3. Add the water, molasses, salt and 1 tablespoon of the soy sauce. Turn the heat to low, cover the pot, and cook gently for 15 minutes.

4. Add the bean sprouts and the almonds, put the cover on, and cook 5 minutes more.

5. In a small bowl, combine the cornstarch and 1 tablespoon of soy sauce to make a paste. Add to the hot vegetables. Cook and stir until the sauce gets thick and just starts to bubble.

TASTY TONGUE
TWISTER:
Say this five
times fast :

SPOCK
SPOTS SPRINGY
SPROUTS

 **Good Sprout Sense**

Sometimes raw sprouts are served on salads and sandwiches. But uncooked sprouts may have germs that can make people sick. Just washing the sprouts in water may not kill all these germs. This is why it is a good idea to cook sprouts before you eat them.

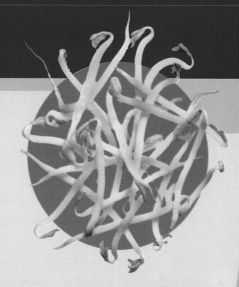

Sprout Farming in a Jar

beans or seeds
l-quart jar
mesh such as plastic screening, cheesecloth, or
clean nylon stocking
canning jar ring or heavy rubber band
water
shallow bowl

1. Put ¼ cup of beans or 2 tablespoons of small sprouting seeds in the jar. Fill the jar to the middle with water. Let this sit on the counter or table for 6 to 12 hours.

2. Cover the mouth of the jar with the mesh. Hold it down with the jar ring or rubber band. Pour out the water carefully, so you don't lose any of the seeds.

3. For the next few days, rinse the seeds through the cover with cool water. Then pour the water out. Do it a second time right away. Shake the jar so the seeds spread out and have room to grow. Do this several times a day. The idea is to keep the seeds damp – but not wet – and to give them plenty of air. The more often sprouts are rinsed, the better they will be.

4. After each rinsing, turn the jar over and let it rest on an angle in a shallow bowl. (See how they are doing it in the pictures on the left.) Store it in a warm, dark place – for example, inside a kitchen cabinet.

5. In 3 to 5 days, when you see tiny tails appear from the seeds, the sprouts are just about done. If you want, you can leave the sprout jar out on the counter for a few hours – just until the tips of the sprouts are a little bit green.

6. When the sprouts are ready, put them in the refrigerator in the sprout jar or in a container that allows some air to get to them. Make sure they are well drained before you store them, so they don't become soggy and start to rot.

7. Eat the sprouts in the next few days. Start another crop right away, so you will always have enough.

Beyond T

ABOUT

Here's a surprise. Tomatoes did not become popular in the United States until the 1800s. People thought they weren't safe to eat, even though they were eaten in South America long before then. Now, they are eaten all over the world. The most flavorful tomatoes are "vine-ripened." Many of the tomatoes in the store are picked too soon. They never taste as sweet as fresh farm or homegrown ripened tomatoes. Even though tomatoes are sold all year long, the best time to buy them is from June through September. Popular types are beefsteak, globe, plum, cherry, yellow cherry, pear tomatoes, and currant tomatoes, which are the tiniest of all. Try them all. In the market, choose firm, well-shaped tomatoes that have a nice color and smell.

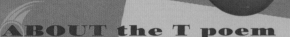

ABOUT the T poem

According to scientists, the tomato is actually a fruit. But most people call it a vegetable and eat it like one. That is why it hangs out with vegetables in places like salads. Watch out! When you tell people a tomato is really a fruit, you may cause a dispute.

Try eating one whole, just like an apple. You'll love it!

Recipe:

Your Own Pita Pizza

1 whole wheat pita bread
6 slices fresh tomato
1/2 cup shredded part skim milk mozzarella cheese
optional: sliced fresh mushrooms, sweet peppers, olives
Parmesan cheese
oregano
olive oil

1. Set the oven or toaster oven to 375°F. and let it warm up.

2. Separate the pita bread into 2 circles. The best way to do this is to punch holes all around the edge with the prongs of a fork. Then gently separate the top and the bottom.

3. Place the bread on a baking sheet with the cut side up.

4. Cover each circle of bread with 3 slices of tomato, 1/4 cup of mozzarella cheese, and any of the vegetables listed here that appeal to you. Feel free to add other vegetables that you think of.

5. Sprinkle some Parmesan cheese and dried oregano evenly on top. Drizzle a little oil over everything.

6. Put the pizza in the oven and bake it for 10 minutes. When the cheese is gooey and the crust is crisp, it is ready.

Amazing Tomatoes

Have you ever seen purple or striped tomatoes? These are two of the many types of tomatoes that are not in the grocery store but were grown at one time. These are called heirloom varieties. You can grow these unusual tomatoes at home in a garden or even in a pot. Get these seeds from: Seed Savers Exchange/ Flower & Herb Exchange, 3094 N. Winn Rd., Decorah, IA 52101 www. seedsaversexchange.org

Tomato Tip

Tomatoes will have the best flavor if you keep them at room temperature, out of direct sunlight. If you have tomatoes that are pale, hard, or still green, you can ripen them at home. You can speed this up by putting them in a closed paper bag. Don't refrigerate tomatoes – unless they are starting to get soft and overripe.

Stopwatch books

Tomato
Barrie Watts

Read On

TOMATO
by Barrie Watts.

(Stopwatch Books, Silver Burdett Press)

You will be amazed to see how tomatoes grow. We love the beautiful color photographs.

Other ways to eat tomatoes

tomato soup

tomato juice

tomato sauce

ketchup

dried tomatoes

tomato paste

ABOUT

It's a grapefruit! It's an orange! It's a tangelo! The Ugli® fruit is a little like all of these. No, not UGLY fruit! They're HOO-GLEE fruit! No one knows for sure how this fruit with this funny name came to be. And not only does it have a funny name, the Ugli® fruit also looks funny, with its green and yellow bumpy skin. But don't judge it by what you see. Inside it is juicy, with a flavor that makes you think of grapefruit – only much sweeter. The Ugli® is in season from winter to spring. They don't grow many Uglis®, so it isn't easy to find them at the store. In the market, choose a fruit that seems heavy and that gives a little when you gently squeeze it. Store it in the refrigerator and eat it within 3 weeks.

Remove the peel with your fingers and eat the sections one at a time.

Recipe:

Ugli® Fruit Salad

Serve this fruit salad as part of a meal. Enough for 4.

1 Ugli® fruit
1 small avocado
½ medium cantaloupe
½ lemon
salt
1 tablespoon honey
½ cup plain, lowfat yogurt

1. Peel the Ugli® fruit. Separate it into sections. Put them in a large salad bowl.

2. Peel the avocado. Cut it into cubes. Add them to the salad bowl.

3. Cut the cantaloupe into cubes or melon balls. Add them to the salad bowl.

4. Squeeze the lemon half over the fruit in the bowl. Add a pinch of salt. Mix well.

5. In a small bowl or jar, beat the honey into the yogurt until you cannot see it any more.

6. Serve the fruit salad on 4 plates. Spoon some of the yogurt dressing on top of each serving.

Uglis® grow here

JAMAICA

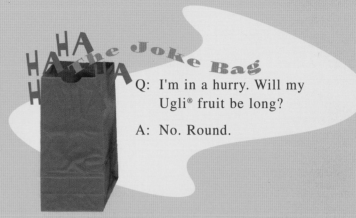

The Joke Bag

HA HA HA HA HA

Q: I'm in a hurry. Will my Ugli® fruit be long?

A: No. Round.

How do you like these hooglies?

The Ugli® comes from the island of Jamaica. Do you see the tiny "®" after the name? The ® is there because the word Ugli is a brand name or registered trademark. That means only one grower can legally use the name Ugli®. Another grower uses the name Uniq® for the same fruit. (By the way, the correct spelling for this word is unique. Unique means "one of a kind." Like you!)

Read On

CITRUS FRUITS

by Susan Wake

(Carolrhoda Books)

Read more about the Ugli® fruit and other citrus fruits, too.

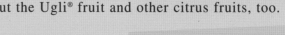

www.ugli.com

Recipes and facts about the fruit with the funny name.

Beyond V

ABOUT The first people to grow vanilla were the Aztec people. The Aztecs ruled part of Mexico more than 800 years ago. They were a very advanced people for their day. Most of the vanilla beans in the world still come from Mexico – plus the island of Madagascar. The vanilla bean grows on a special orchid. On the page with the vanilla poem you can see the orchid in the poster. There are more than 30,000 kinds of orchids, but this is the only one that produces anything you can eat. This is lucky for us, since vanilla is one of the most popular flavors in the world. The vanilla flavor is obtained from the seeds inside the bean. But most people use something called vanilla extract, which is made from these seeds. Many stores sell imitation vanilla. This is made from chemicals that taste and smell like vanilla, but there is no real vanilla bean in it.

Recipes:

Vanilla Oatmeal

Here is a new way to flavor your breakfast cereal.

    oatmeal
    1 vanilla bean pod cut into pieces

1. Mix the cut-up vanilla bean into the oatmeal in its box or other container. Store for at least 2 weeks before using.

2. When you want some oatmeal, remove the oats and cook them in the usual way. Leave the vanilla bean pieces in the container.

3. When you have cooked and eaten all the oatmeal, refill the container with new oats. You can use the same vanilla beans to flavor two or three refills.

Priscilla's Vanilla Pudding

Makes 4 bowls.

    3 tablespoons cornstarch
    2 cups lowfat milk
    ¼ cup honey
    1 teaspoon vanilla extract

1. In a bowl, stir the cornstarch into ¼ cup of the milk, until it is completely mixed in.

2. In a 1-quart pot, combine the remaining 1³/₄ cups milk and the honey. Cook this over medium heat, until it is very hot, but not boiling.

3. Turn the heat under the pot to low. Add the cornstarch-milk mixture. Cook until the pudding is thick and starts to boil, stirring gently all the time with a wooden spoon. Boil gently for 30 seconds.

4. Remove the pudding from the heat. Stir in the vanilla extract.

5. Spoon the pudding into 4 dessert bowls. Let it cool to room temperature. Then put the bowls in the refrigerator. Eat when cold.

Vanilla grows here

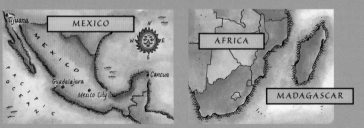

Vanilla Figs

This special dessert will feed 4 to 6 people. If you want to be really fancy, put a small scoop of vanilla ice cream on top of each serving.

    12 dried golden figs
    2 tablespoons raisins
    1¼ cups apple juice
    1 vanilla bean pod, split lengthwise
    2 tablespoons lemon juice

1. Combine the figs, raisins, and apple juice in a pot. Scrape the vanilla beans out of the pod and into the pot.

2. Bring to a boil and cook for just 1 minute.

3. Remove the pot from the stove. Pour everything into a bowl. Stir in the lemon juice.

4. Refrigerate the bowl of figs for several hours. You can even prepare this a day or two ahead.

5. For each serving, cut 2 or 3 figs into bite-size pieces. Place in serving dishes.

6. Remove the vanilla beans from the syrup. Spoon some syrup and some raisins onto each dish of figs. Serve just as it is, or with some vanilla ice cream on top.

Visit an Orchid

If you want to see the kind of plant that the vanilla bean grows on – you can. Beautiful orchids can be found in many flower shops, greenhouses, and botanical gardens.

Read On

GROWING UP IN AZTEC TIMES

by Richard Hook

(Troll)

How these amazing people lived – especially their young people.

·GROWING UP IN· **Aztec Times** MARION WOOD

True Food **Fact**

Vanilla in your brownies? Yup. Vanilla is often used in making chocolate treats like ice cream, cakes, and hot chocolate. Why? Because vanilla makes the chocolate taste better.

ABOUT the V picture

The vanilla bean is not the kind of bean most people think of when they hear the word "bean." More people know green beans or the dried beans that are used in soups and stews. The flavor called vanilla also comes from a bean. Of course, you do not eat the bean pod the way it looks in this scoop of ice cream. But if you look closely, sometimes you do see black specks from vanilla beans in vanilla ice cream.

To see vanilla plants and learn to say vanilla in 52 different languages

WWW.uni-graz.at/~katzer/engl/Vani_pla.html

Beyond W

ABOUT The first watermelons came from South Africa. Today they are grown in 90 countries. The United States is the fourth largest grower. Most watermelons are red inside, but they come pink, orange, yellow, and white, too. There are even seedless watermelons. But then you miss the fun of spitting out the seeds. Do you know how to tell if a watermelon is ready to eat? Slap it! A high sound means it is not ripe. A dull thud means it is too ripe. A deep sound means it is just right. Make sure you buy a ripe one, since watermelons do not get riper once they are off the vine.

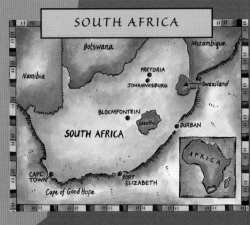

SOUTH AFRICA

Botswana
Mozambique
Namibia
PRETORIA
JOHANNESBURG
Swaziland
BLOEMFONTEIN
Lesotho
DURBAN
SOUTH AFRICA
AFRICA
CAPE TOWN
PORT ELIZABETH
Cape of Good Hope

OOH!

Make sure you have a place to spit out the seeds. The world record for seed spitting is said to be 68 feet, 11 inches! It is held by Jack Dietz of Chicago, Illinois.

Recipe:

Watermelon Shake

A shake for 4 to drink – or freeze some for a treat you can eat.

2 cups watermelon cubes
1 pint fresh strawberries, washed, stems removed
1 banana, peeled and sliced
8-ounce container vanilla or lemon lowfat yogurt

1. Remove the pits from the watermelon.

2. In a blender or food processor, combine all the ingredients. Run the machine until everything is smooth and foamy.

3. Pour the shake into 4 tall glasses to drink right away. Or turn it into Frozen Watermelon Treats (see step 4).

4. Frozen Watermelon Treats: Pour the Watermelon Shake into 4- or 6-ounce paper cups and place them in the freezer. When partially frozen (about 1½ hours), insert ice pop sticks or plastic spoons. Freeze until hard. Peel off the paper cup before eating.

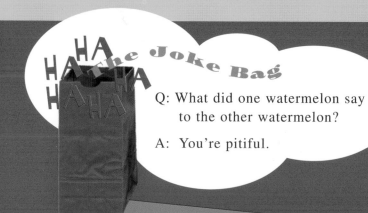

The Joke Bag

Q: What did one watermelon say to the other watermelon?

A: You're pitiful.

Watermelon Poem

The round supreme and celestial watermelon.

It is the fruit of the tree of thirst,

It is the green whale of summer.

– Pablo Neruda

Kathi Appelt

WATERMELON DAY

Illustrated by Dale Gottlieb

Read On

WATERMELON DAY

by Kathi Appelt.

(Henry Holt and Co.)

Young readers can join Jesse as he watches a watermelon grow throughout the summer, until it is finally ready to pick and enjoy.

www. watermelon.org/kids.asp

Growing instructions plus puzzles, science, puppets, and a coloring book.

True Food Fact

Watermelons are 91% water. The biggest watermelon ever grown was said to be 268.8 feet by Lloyd Bright of Arkansas.

Beyond X

ABOUT Xemenia is a small, round, yellow plum from Africa. It is a wild fruit. This does not mean that the fruit gets into trouble or runs wild, as in the picture. It means it is not grown on farms. You can only find xemenia where this bush happens to grow, so it's unlikely you will get to eat one. The reason we included xemenia in this book is because we needed a fruit or vegetable that begins with the letter X. The xemenia is also a good reminder that there are many fruits and vegetables in the world that are not well known. If you travel to other countries, you might find some fruits and vegetables that are not grown where you live. Be an adventurer and try new foods.

Wild Food

The fruits and vegetables that grow on farms and in gardens once grew wild. There are still plenty of plants that grow wild that are good to eat. Some are found in the woods and open fields. Some grow in empty lots, even in cities. Others grow like weeds on lawns and in gardens. Here are some: blackberries, wild strawberries, crab apples, watercress, purslane, sorrel, day lily buds, violets, mint, wild onions. See if you can find an expert in your area to take you on a tour. Never forget, not all plants are safe to eat. Do not taste anything unless an expert has told you it's okay.

Want to see something wild?

In the United States you can see the xemenia and lots of other unusual plants at the Rare Fruit & Spice Park in Homestead, Florida. The park is about one hour from Miami. You can see photos of the park at

www.fruitandspicepark.org

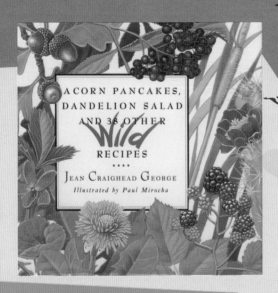

ACORN PANCAKES,
DANDELION SALAD
AND 38 OTHER
Wild
RECIPES
••••
JEAN CRAIGHEAD GEORGE
Illustrated by Paul Mirocha

Read On

**ACORN PANCAKES,
DANDELION SALAD AND
33 OTHER WILD RECIPES**
by Jean Craighead George.
(HarperCollins)

Recipes for some wild foods that you
might find in your own
neighborhood.

How Do You Like These X's?

If you have X's in a row,
Then you're playing tic-tac-toe.

If a big X marks the spot,
Then buried treasure's what you've got.

If your name you cannot sign,
Make your X above the line.

In ancient Rome, the X meant ten –
It's just the way they did it then.

An X in math can signify
That it's time to multiply.

And sometimes when you take a quiz,
You have to find out what X is.

Often when you take a test,
You mark the proper box with X.

A jar with X's says beware –
Three of them means poison's there.

An X is often warning you
A railroad train is coming through.

When X's for the eyes are painted
In comics, that means someone's fainted.

When writing someone whom you miss,
The letter X stands for a kiss.

Beyond Y

ABOUT Africa is the home of the first yams. Yams also grow in South and Central America and the West Indies. In the United States, some people think yams and sweet potatoes are the same. Not so. While they look and taste similar, they are different vegetables. If you want to try real yams, you can often find them in natural food stores or markets where Spanish-speaking people shop. In the market, select yams with unwrinkled skins and no soft or discolored spots. Store in a place that is cool, dark, and dry for up to 2 weeks. Do not refrigerate. By the way, if a recipe calls for yams and you cannot find them, you can use sweet potatoes instead.

ABOUT the Y poem and picture

Most people cannot tell a yam from a sweet potato. In many food stores, a kind of sweet potato is often called a yam, even though it isn't. If you see a sign for yams in the market, ask about them. Join the wise people in the poem and discover the truth. (We bet they are sweet potatoes!)

Do you know the geniuses in the picture? From left to right: Albert Einstein was one of the greatest mathematicians who ever lived; Sir Isaac Newton, one of the greatest scientists; Groucho Marx, one of the greatest comics; and Plato, one of the greatest thinkers.

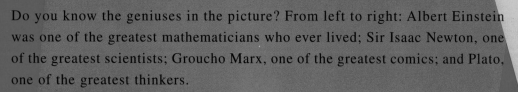

AFRICA

Recipes:

Candied Yams

This recipe feeds 6 to 8.
Leftovers make a great snack.

> 2 pounds yams or sweet potatoes
> 2 tablespoons maple syrup
> ½ cup apple juice
> ¼ teaspoon salt
> 1 tablespoon butter
> ½ cup chopped pecans

1. Set the oven to 350°F. and let it warm up.

2. Peel the yams or sweet potatoes. Cut them into slices ¼ inch thick.

3. In a shallow 2-quart baking dish, combine the yams or sweet potatoes, maple syrup, apple juice, and salt.

4. Cut the butter into tiny pieces. Use them to dot the tops of the yams.

5. Cover the baking dish. Put it in the oven for 45 minutes, or until the yams are tender.

6. Take the cover off the baking dish. Scatter the nuts all over the top. Put it back in the oven for 15 minutes.

Pot-of-Gold Biscuits

¼ pound yam or sweet potato
2 cups whole wheat flour
2 teaspoons baking powder
¼ teaspoon baking soda
½ teaspoon salt
¼ cup oil
½ cup orange juice
1 tablespoon honey

1. Set the oven to 425°F. and let it warm up.

2. Peel the yam or sweet potato. Shred it on a box grater or in a food processor. You should have about ¾ cup.

3. In a bowl, mix together the flour, baking powder, baking soda, and salt.

4. Stir the oil into the flour mixture until it disappears.

5. Stir the shredded yam or sweet potato into the flour mixture.

6. Add the juice and the honey to the flour mixture. Stir with a spoon, until all the flour is wet and you have a smooth dough.

7. When you have mixed it as much as you can, squish the dough together with your hands a few times, so that it sticks together. This is called "kneading."

8. Dampen a paper towel with oil. Use it to oil a cookie sheet or a large baking pan.

9. Place the biscuit dough on the oiled baking pan. Pat it so that it is about ½ inch thick. Cut it into 12 squares that are each about 1½ inches. Moving them 1-inch apart will make them crisper.

10. Bake the biscuits for 12 to 15 minutes, until they are golden brown.

True Food Fact

Some yams are giants. They grow as long as 7½ feet and can weigh as much as 120 pounds.

NOTHING ELSE BUT YAMS FOR SUPPER!

Story by Joan Buchanan   Illustrations by Jirina Marton

Read On

NOTHING ELSE BUT YAMS FOR SUPPER
by Joan Buchanan

(Black Moss Press)

Beginning readers can travel around the world with a young girl as she discovers other foods she likes to eat as much as yams.

Tongue Twister

Say this five times fast:

Ma'am, I am a yam

Growing a Yam Tree

Yams (and sweet potatoes) grow to become fantastic-looking plants, like the one above. To grow one, you must use a yam or potato that has not been coated with wax. Just put it in a dark place and wait a few weeks. Watch as sprouts grow out. You can plant it in a pot, half buried, for a long-lasting plant. Keep the plant watered.

Beyond Z

ABOUT This popular summer vegetable was first grown in South America. It is a type of squash. The Indians in South America who first grew squash called it "askutasquash," which means "green thing eaten green." The zucchini's skin can be dark to light green. Sometimes it has yellow markings that give it a freckled or striped look. Fresh zucchini is available all year in most markets, but it is really in season from late spring through summer. In the market, select zucchinis that are about 6 to 8 inches long. They are the most tender and sweet. When zucchinis grow too big, their skins get tough and the insides become watery. The skin on zucchinis should look clean and have a bright color. Store in a cool place.

How do you like these squash?

Zucchini is part of the squash family. Some squash, like zucchini, are called summer squash because they are picked in warm weather and only keep for a few days. Yellow crookneck, patty pan, and spaghetti squash are all summer squash you should try. Winter squash are ready to pick at the end of the summer and fall. They have a harder shell and can sometimes be stored for months. Most winter squash are sweet. Acorn squash, butternut squash, hubbard squash, and sugar or pie pumpkin are all winter squash. Try 'em all.

Eat a fresh zucchini. Pretend it's a long green apple.

Zucchini with Linguini

Dinner for 4.

- ½ pound linguini
- 2 tablespoons olive oil
- 1 large clove garlic, chopped
- 4 scallions, thinly sliced
- ½ cup diced sweet red pepper
- 1 pound zucchini
- 2 medium tomatoes, chopped
- 1 tablespoon chopped fresh basil
- ¼ cup chopped fresh parsley

1. Bring a large pot of water to boil for the linguini. Cook it while you prepare the sauce.

2. Heat the oil in a large frying pan. Add the garlic, scallions, and red pepper. Cook for 2 to 3 minutes, until lightly colored.

3. Shred the zucchini, using a box grater or food processor. Add the zucchini, tomatoes, basil, and parsley to the frying pan. Cook for about 5 minutes, until the zucchini is soft and the sauce is hot.

4. When the linguini is cooked to taste, put it in a serving bowl. Spoon the zucchini sauce over the linguini and serve.

Z's Mystery Cake

No one will ever guess the secret ingredient!

1¼ cups whole wheat pastry flour

⅓ cup carob powder

½ teaspoon baking soda

¼ teaspoon salt

1¼ cups lightly packed, shredded zucchini

¼ cup oil

⅓ cup honey

1 egg

½ teaspoon vanilla extract

¼ cup plain yogurt

¼ cup carob chips or chocolate chips

1. Set the oven to 350°F and let it warm up.

2. In a large bowl, mix together the flour, carob powder, baking soda, salt, and shredded zucchini.

3. In separate bowl, beat together the oil, honey, egg, and vanilla.

4. Gently stir the egg mixture into the flour mixture until it is no longer dry.

5. Stir in the yogurt until it is completely mixed in.

6. Dampen a paper towel with oil and use it to wipe an 8-inch square baking pan.

7. Spread the cake batter into the baking pan.

8. Scatter the chips evenly over the top.

9. Bake the cake for 30 to 35 minutes. When it is done, it will feel firm in the middle when you press it gently with your fingers.

10. Wait until the cake cools before you cut a piece.

LAURIE KRASNY BROWN

THE VEGETABLE SHOW

Read On

THE VEGETABLE SHOW

by Laurie Krasny Brown

(Little, Brown)

Vegetables put on a stage show to show off their talent to kids of all ages.

A Funny Holiday

Zucchini grow very easily and gardeners often end up with too many. Growers sometimes even have trouble giving them away! Because of this, a man named Thomas Roy has created this funny holiday, "Sneak Some Zucchini Onto Your Neighbor's Porch Night." On August 8th, people find nice ways to give away their extra zucchini, such as leaving them on neighbors' porches and in their cars. It is observed in Roy's hometown of Mount Gretna, Pennsylvania, and more places worldwide. Do you have extra zucchini? Why not share the harvest by finding nice ways to give them away?

True Food Fact

In 1998, a man in England grew the largest known squash – 135 pounds!

www.zucchinibrothers.com
A bunch of wild and crazy songs.

OTHER BOOKS BY NIKKI & DAVID GOLDBECK

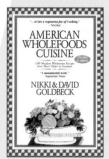

AMERICAN WHOLE-FOODS CUISINE/*Over 1,300 Meatless, Wholesome Recipes from Short Order to Gourmet* A classic of contemporary vegetarian cooking, plus 300 pages of valuable kitchen information. Considered "the new *Joy of Cooking*" by authorities from Food & Wine to Vegetarian Times. Over 250,000 in print. *(580 pages/Paper)* $21.95

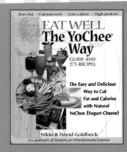

EAT WELL THE YOCHEE WAY Enjoy rich creamy dishes without the fat and calories. High-protein, calcium-rich YoChee (yogurt cheese) is the ideal substitute for cream cheese, sour cream or mayonnaise. Improve your diet without forgoing your favorite dishes. Simple directions and 275 recipes. *(310 pages/Paper)* Also, YoChee makers (available online). $18.95

CHOOSE TO REUSE/*An Encyclopedia of Services, Products, Programs & Charitable Organizations That Foster Reuse.* This revolutionary guide is the first to show the ingenious ways that individuals, businesses and charitable organizations can profit from reuse—the second environmental "R." More than 200 topics and 2,000 resources from Air Filters to Zippers. A Book-of-the-Month Club selection. *(480 pages/Paper)* $10.95

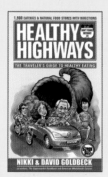

HEALTHY HIGHWAYS/*The Travelers' Guide to Healthy Eating* State maps and local directions guide you to 1,900 healthy eateries and natural food stores throughout the U.S. Plus travel tips, dining advice and other useful resources. Free online supplement keeps the book up to date.

(420 pages/Paper) $18.95

THE GOOD BREAKFAST BOOK 450 vegetarian recipes to jumpstart the day. Quick weekday getaways to elegant brunches. Great for families. Includes recipes suitable for vegans, as well as people with wheat, dairy and egg sensitivities. *(206 pages/Paper)* $9.95

THE ABC'S OF FRUITS AND VEGETABLES AND BEYOND/*Delicious Alphabet Poems plus Food, Facts and Fun for Everyone.* A collaboration of Steve Charney and David Goldbeck. Actually two books in one. In Part One, the ABCs are taught via twenty-six funny and clever fruit and vegetable poems. Part Two continues to delight older children with a mix of fruit and vegetable jokes, tongue twisters, fun facts, kid-friendly recipes, shopping tips, and more. *(112 pages/ Illustrated/Color throughout/Paper)* $16.95

ORDER VIA THE WEB, MAIL, FAX OR PHONE

Ceres Press • PO Box 87 • Dept ABC • Woodstock, NY 12498

Phone/FAX 845-679-5573

visit **wwww.HealthyHighways.com** for online specials

For More About Steve Charney's Books and Performances Visit wwww.stevecharney.com

Steve Charney

Steve Charney is a nationally known children's entertainer, magician, ventriloquist, songwriter, and radio personality. His books include *Hocus Jokus* and *Kid's Kookiest Riddles*. He is also the co-host, with his dummy Harry, of the radio program *Knock On Wood*. Steve performs at festivals, theaters, and libraries throughout the world and Steve and Harry often promote literacy in schools as well. He has written dozens of songs for Jim Henson's TV show *Bear in the Big Blue House*. Steve eats lots of fruits and vegetables in the beautiful Hudson Valley with his wife, Elise, and his dummy, Harry. His website is www. stevecharney.com

David Goldbeck

David Goldbeck is co-author with Nikki Goldbeck of nine food books. These books include the best-sellers, *The Supermarket Handbook, American Wholefoods Cuisine* and, most recently, *Healthy Highways*. He is the author of *The Smart Kitchen*. David, trained as a lawyer, has worked as a waiter, produce man, and elementary school teacher. He, too, eats his fruits and vegetables while enjoying the Catskill Mountains in New York's Hudson Valley. His website is www.HealthyHighways.com

Maria Burgaleta Larson

Maria Burgaleta Larson grew up in New York City and spent her childhood summers in Cuba. She is a graduate of The Cooper Union and a Fellow of The American Academy in Rome.

CERES PRESS

BOOKS THAT MAKE A DIFFERENCE SINCE 1977
PO Box 87 Dept. ABC, Woodstock, NY 12498 USA
(845) 679-5573 • cem620@aol.com • www.HealthyHighways.com